The bumper book of
Horses and Ponies

Janet Rising

A HORSE'S MOUTH PUBLICATION

First published in Great Britain in 2002
© **D J Murphy (Publishers) Ltd**
The Horse's Mouth is a subsidiary of
D J Murphy (Publishers) Ltd

Text © Janet Rising
Janet Rising has asserted her right under the Copyright, Designs
and Patents Act 1988 to be identified as the author of this work.

Design: **Jamie Powell**

Published by **D J Murphy (Publishers) Ltd,**
Haslemere House, Lower Street, Haslemere,
Surrey GU27 2PE.
Origination by **Ford Graphics**, Ltd, Ringwood,
Hampshire.
Printed by **The Grange Press**, Brighton,
West Sussex.

ISBN 0-9513707-4-X

Credits
Front cover images:
Only Horses Picture Library & Janet Rising.

Photography credits
Bob Langrish pages 8, 9, 12, 13, 23, 30, 31, 38, 52, 53, 58, 59,
70, 71, 77, 88 & 89.
David Miller pages 16, 17, 22, 24, 25, 60, 61 & 98.
Janet Rising pages 5, 14, 15, 32, 33, 38, 39, 48, 49, 62, 63, 72,
73, 74, 78, 79, 82, 83, 86 & 87.
Nicky Moffatt page 67.

Artwork
Helena Öhmark and Rebecca Enström pages 10, 11, 28, 29, 36,
37, 40, 41, 46, 47, 54, 55, 80 & 81.
Horse's Mouth logo by **Anne Pilgrim**.

How to get the most out of
The Bumper Book of Horses and Ponies

Horses and ponies have always fascinated humans. They are graceful, fast, beautiful and they have helped us throughout history in travel, agriculture, industry and war. Their history is our history.

This book has lots of information about horses and ponies - breed files, riding information and stable management features. There is also a great deal of general horsy knowledge, such as pages about the farrier and the vet - and even some great horsy things to make yourself.

You can have a great time simply learning about horses and ponies, or you can really put your reading and new knowledge to the test! There are four double pages of quizzes in the book - all entitled *Test Yourself* - and the quizzes are all about the pages preceding them. So, the quiz on pages 26 and 27 has questions all about the information you will have read between pages 8 and 25.

If you want to get the most out of *The Bumper Book of Horses and Ponies*, read each page in the right order, then try the quiz after each section. There are spaces to write your answers on the quiz pages so if you write in pencil (or use a separate sheet of paper, noting down the numbers of the questions) you can add up your score, then do the quiz again until you get every single question right. The answers to all the quiz questions are on pages 96 and 97 - so don't turn to these pages until you have read the whole book!

There are also puzzles to do - and the answers to these are on pages 94 and 95. The puzzle answers don't count towards the quiz questions, so you can do these whenever you want to.

We hope you have a great time reading *The Bumper Book of Horses and Ponie*s. And we hope you enjoy answering the quiz questions, too.

So, what are you waiting for? Start reading!

Contents

poll

ear

crest

forelock

nostril

muzzle

throat

mouth & lips

cheek

chin groove

shoulder

Points of the horse

Every part of the horse has its own unique name. See how many you can learn, as knowing these points always comes in handy when you are talking about horses, or learning to ride. That way, you will know what everyone is talking about!

elbow

knee

chestnut

coronet

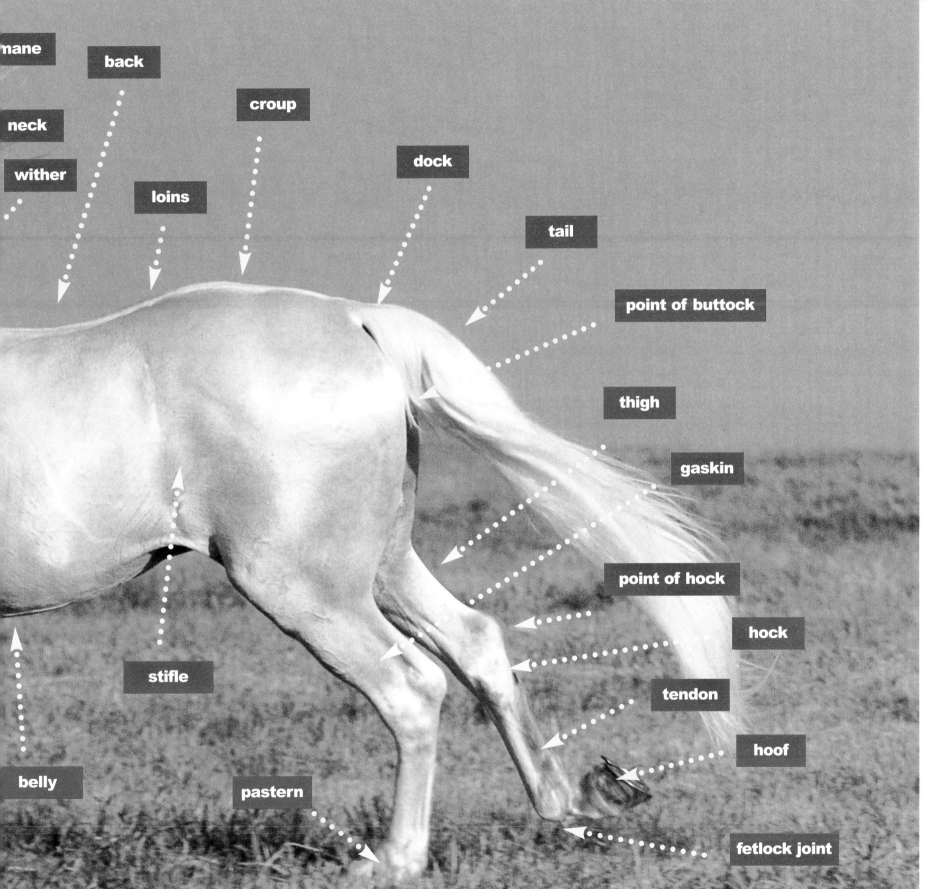

mane

back

neck

croup

wither

dock

loins

tail

point of buttock

thigh

gaskin

point of hock

hock

stifle

tendon

belly

hoof

pastern

fetlock joint

The walk

What happens when we ask a pony to walk?
Here's the answer!

Four beats

The walk is a pace of four-time. This means that for every full stride the pony makes, he puts each of his feet down on the ground separately, making four beats. The beats are regular so, when you listen to the foot falls your pony makes as he walks, you will hear the beats one-two-three-four, one-two-three-four. The walk should be purposeful (not wandering along as though in a daze) and, if you concentrate, you can feel the movement of each foot underneath you!

Overtracking

If your pony is moving well and actively, his hind feet should actually overtrack his front feet - making a longer stride.

Aids to walk

To ask your pony to walk from halt, close your legs around his sides to ask him to move on,

Foot falls

Here you can see each of the four foot-falls at walk. Obviously, the pony has more than one foot on the ground at all times, but the hoof marked is the one making the beat.

Did you know?
Racehorse trainers say that if a racehorse has a long-striding walk which covers the ground, he will also be able to gallop really fast!

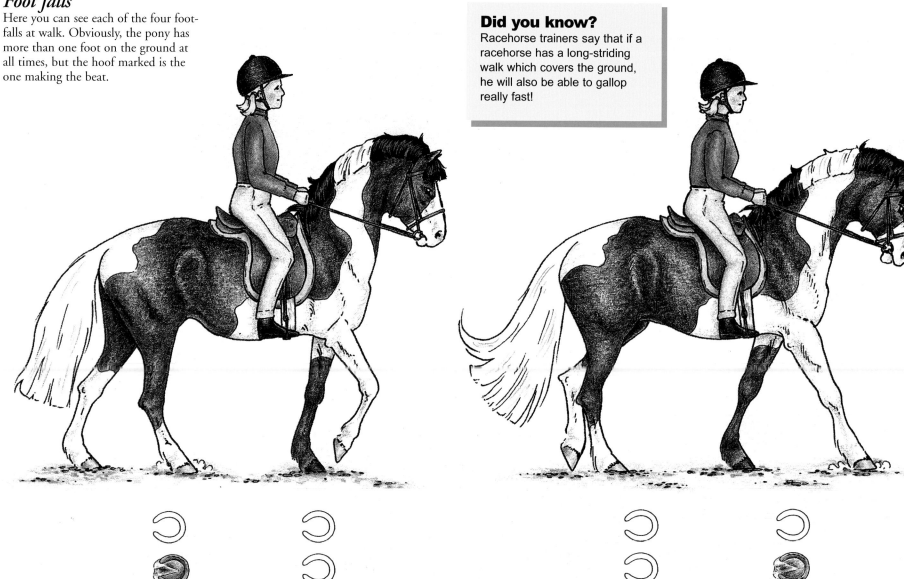

allowing your hand forward without losing your contact with his mouth through the reins. As your pony walks on, keep your back supple and allow your body to go with the movement, without creating any movement of your own.

Walking up and down hills

A horse or pony carries two-thirds of its own bodyweight on its front legs, so when you go up and down hills, it helps your pony if you lean forward slightly, to keep your own weight over his front legs.

Why don't you?

Take a look at horses and ponies walking next time you watch a lesson. See which ones are overtracking and which ones are not and whether the beats to the walk are regular. See if you can tell which pony is walking well! It can be tricky trying to see the legs and sorting out the beats to the stride - but with practice you will do it!

Did you know?

There are many different kinds of walk. Collected walk is where the rider has the horse walking with short, high steps, with plenty of energy. The opposite to this would be a free walk on a long rein, where the rider lengthens the reins and allows the horse to stretch his neck down and have a rest.

The Arabian

The Arabian horse makes a striking sight. With flowing mane and tail and graceful, floating action, the Arab horse is unique in the horse world. Read on to discover more about this beautiful horse.

History

Records of Arabian horses date back as long ago as 3000 years! Arab Bedouin tribes bred their horses with great care - and they were so valuable that they shared their tents with them. This ensured that the breed had a good temperament and had great affinity with their owners who, in turn, prized them highly. Imagine living with an Arabian horse in your house!

Legend

Legend has it that when God decided to create horse he condensed the South wind. With a handful of this substance God fashioned a chestnut horse and hung happiness from its forelock. Lord of the other animals, the Arabian horse was bestowed with men who followed him, riches and great fortune. Finally, God gave his creation the mark of glory and happiness, a white mark on his forehead which many Arabians have today.

Why Arabs are famous

Arabians are famous for their stamina, speed and beauty. It is considered that the Arabian horse is perfect - and that man cannot improve on it. This is why Arabians in Great Britain are never trimmed. Their manes and tails are left long and flowing, their whiskers kept intact. It takes some effort to keep an Arabian horse looking good. Just think of the hard work keeping tangles out of that long mane and tail!

Influence

The Arabian has been influential in almost every breed of horse - including the heavy Percheron from France! There are several different types of Arabian - although they all share the characteristics of a dished face, wide forehead, large nostrils and high tail carriage. The Arabian is unmistakable!

Arabian factoid
Arabian horses have 17 ribs, five lumber vertebrae (bones in their back) and 16 tail bones. All other horses have 18 ribs, six lumber vertebrae and 18 tail bones!

How to spot an Arabian

Originated in: Middle Eastern deserts.
Colours: Grey, chestnut, bay or black.
Height: Between 14hh - 15.2hh.
How to spot an Arabian: Wide forehead, big eyes, small ears, large nostrils and an arched neck all make the Arabian easy to spot.
Good at: Arabians excel at anything which demands speed, stamina and courage. This is why so many top long-distance horses are Arabians!
Is an Arabian for you? Arabians make great mounts for people who can give them loyalty and love - and they return it. They often relate to only one person, so if you want a horse which looks beautiful, has courage and speed, and will love you forever, the Arabian is for you!

Arabian factoid
Arabian horses have a distinct floating action when they trot - they appear to hang in the air between strides. They also hold their heads high, with their nostrils flared wide. This action is known as drinking the wind and is thought to keep the Arabian's head above the dust of the desert, helping him to breathe.

Arabian factoid
Even though Arabian horses may sometimes be small, they are always referred to as horses, never as ponies.

Get grooming!

Grooming is not only a great way to keep your pony clean, it also gives you an opportunity to check him all over, and allows you to get more acquainted!

Grooming kit
If you are to get a clean pony, your grooming kit needs to be kept clean! Keep it all together in a special box or carrier, and try not to use it on any other pony.

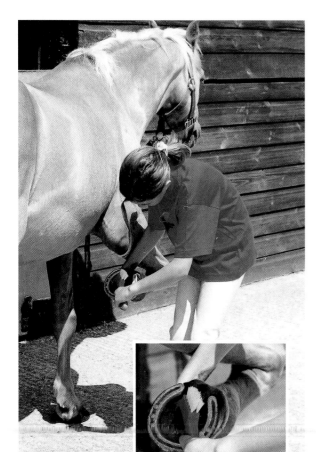

Just dandy!
The dandy brush has long, stiff bristles and is used to remove dried mud and sweat. Do not use it on the mane and tail however, as it can break the hairs. Use the dandy brush briskly, but be careful on bony parts, and wherever the pony may be ticklish.

Hooves first!
Start with the hoofpick. Your pony's feet need to be clean to keep them healthy - and you can also check his shoes at the same time. Use the hoofpick from heel to toe; this prevents you from digging the frog, the spongy triangular bit under the hoof. Hold the hoof, not the pony's leg, as it will seem much lighter. Once the hoofpick has got the hoof clean, you can turn the hoofpick around and brush out the hoof to get it really clean!

Two at once
The body brush has a handle and short, soft bristles which get right into the coat and remove the grease. For this reason, the body brush needs to be used with a metal curry comb - the curry comb cleans the body brush, and is never used on the pony. Use short stokes, drawing the brush over the curry comb every fourth or fifth stroke. To clean the curry comb, tap it on the ground away from the pony.

Manes and tails

The body brush is also the brush to use on your pony's mane and tail - as well as his face. When you brush the tail, remember to stand to one side and brush a few hairs at a time. Use a dampened water brush to lay the mane flat.

Did you know?

Ponies which live out in the field need the grease in their coat as it protects them against the rain - a bit like a rainmac. For this reason, you should only use a dandy brush on their coat, using the body brush for their face, mane and tail, only. Use a body brush on stable-kept ponies, instead.

Did you know?

You should always tie up your pony before you groom him, to prevent him from wandering about. Make sure you tie him up short - this is known as *short racking*.

Did you know?

You should never kneel down around your pony. Always bend down instead. Then, if anything frightens your pony, you can get up very quickly and get yourself out of the way!

There - one smart pony!

A bit of a wash

Dampen the sponge and clean around your pony's eyes, nose and dock. You might like to use separate sponges for the face, and under the tail - much nicer!

Hooves last!

Finally, you can paint some hoof oil onto the hooves to make them shine.

Why don't you?

If you haven't got a pony of your own, why not see if you can get your own grooming kit to clean your favourite riding school pony? That way, you will always have a brush to hand!

In the saddle
The rider's position

How you sit in the saddle is very important. You need to be safe. You need to be balanced. You need to be able to communicate with your pony. Here is a list of things to remember as you maintain a good riding position.

◆ Sit tall. Keep your back straight. Think about the top half of you growing upwards, the bottom half of you growing downwards.

◆ Look up and ahead. Never look down or tilt your head to one side as this affects your whole position.

◆ See if you can feel both your seat bones. Make sure your weight is equal on each one.

◆ Carry your own hands. Don't let them rest on your pony's neck or on the saddle as this will pull your shoulders down, bringing your head with them.

◆ Allow your legs to hang close to your pony's sides.

◆ Allow your weight to drop down through your leg to your heel - without pushing down.

Line up!
There should be a straight line from your ear, through your shoulder and hip, down to your heel. This way you are in a balanced position. This makes it easy for you to stay in position, and for your pony to carry you.

There should also be a straight line from your elbow, through your hands, along the reins to the bit in your pony's mouth.

Top tips for a good position
It is important to stay relaxed in the saddle, even though you are in this position. That way, when your pony moves you will move with him and maintain your position, instead of getting left behind.

Remember how it feels
Once you have the correct position, try to remember how it feels. It may seem a little strange at first, but after a while you should be able to keep your correct riding position without too much effort.

Follow the movement
As your pony moves, let yourself follow the movement.

Correct yourself
As you ask your pony to go faster, or slow down and stop, you may find that your position alters. As you feel this happening, see if you can correct yourself before your instructor notices.

Riding like a natural
After a while you should be able to keep your great riding position without thinking about it!

Riding on the lunge

Until you are secure in the saddle and have a good position, you may be taught on the lunge. This long line allows your instructor to control the pony - and allows you to concentrate on yourself!

Once you are allowed off the lunge line, not only will you need to keep your riding position, you will also need to tell the pony what you want him to do. Don't worry, you'll soon get the hang of it!

Bridles

The bridle allows the rider to communicate with their horse, using the reins. A bit, worn in the mouth, gives the rider control over the horse, but it is important to remember that the mouth is sensitive, and easily bruised. Read on to discover more about bridles!

All about teeth

The horse has two different sets of teeth; the *incisors*, at the front, graze grass and find food, which is then pushed to the back of the mouth by the tongue. The back teeth, the *molars*, go a very long way along the skull, almost level with the horse's eye! These molars grind up the food, making it ready to swallow. Between the two sets of teeth is a gap, and it is in this gap that the bit lies. This gap helps us to put the bridle on - we can put a thumb in the corner without fear of being bitten!

Parts of a bridle

This simple snaffle bridle - taken from the name of the snaffle bit - has a single rein. Can you memorise all the parts of the bridle?

headpiece

browband

throatlatch

cheekpiece

noseband

bit

reins

The double bridle

This bridle is quite complicated - it has two separate bits in the horse's mouth. Called a double bridle, the two bits are a snaffle - called a *bridoon*, and a curb, called a *weymouth*. Each bit works on different parts of the horse's head and mouth. It can only be used by very experienced riders, and on horses which are well schooled. Not only does it have two bits, it has a curb chain, which acts on the chin groove. A double bridle takes some practice to put on and fit correctly!

The Pelham

If a horse or pony doesn't get on with two bits, there is a bit called a Pelham, which is just a single mouthpiece, but with two rings on it to take two pairs of reins. The curb rein, on the bottom ring, acts like a curb bit and works on the horse's poll.

The top rein acts like a snaffle. So the rider has greater control, but the horse only has a single bit!

Noseband variety

This horse is wearing a snaffle bit, but he has a different noseband on. This flash noseband goes under the bit and gives the rider extra control if their horse goes too fast. This might happen when they ride across country or around a set of show jumps.

Bit variety

This pony is wearing a snaffle - but it is a special type, called a Fulmer snaffle. The bars on either side help to guide a young horse or pony when the rider uses the reins to ask the pony to turn.

Specialist bridles

This bridle has fancy brass buckles and a chain on the bit which allows a lead rein to be attached. This bridle is for showing the horse in-hand at a horse show. In-hand classes are where horses and ponies are shown by being led around the ring, instead of being ridden. This bridle really looks smart and makes the horse look very special!

Did you know?
The name for a person who makes bits for bridles is called a *Loriner*.

Cowboy story

Western horses wear different tack to horses ridden English style. This Quarter Horse has an ornate one-ear bridle. Instead of a browband, the bridle has an extra piece around one ear which prevents the headpiece from slipping back. The bit is different, too, with a single rein on a curb bit. This bridle is for competition work - just look at the silver on it!

Did you know?
Bits can be made from a variety of materials including stainless steel, copper, rubber and a special plastic, called *vulcanite*.

Did you know?
The knights of old had very long curb bits on their enormous horses. They needed lots of control. They could be as long as 38cms long! These bits were not exactly kind as they exerted great force.

Did you know?
You don't have to use a bit! There are bitless bridles on the market - and these work by applying pressure on the horse's nose. They may seem to be kinder than a bridle with a bit, but they can restrict a horse's breathing, and need to be used by very experienced riders.

Why don't you?

The next time you go to a horse show, or visit a riding school, why not see how many different bits and bridles you can see? If you see one you don't recognise, ask the rider about it. That way, you will learn even more about bits and bridles.

Puzzle fun!

How many of our great horsy puzzles can you solve?

Square by square

Can you draw this pony by copying square by square?

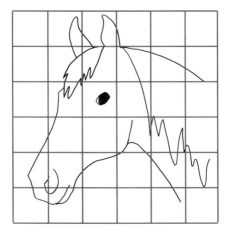

Odd one out

Which of these is the odd one out – and why?

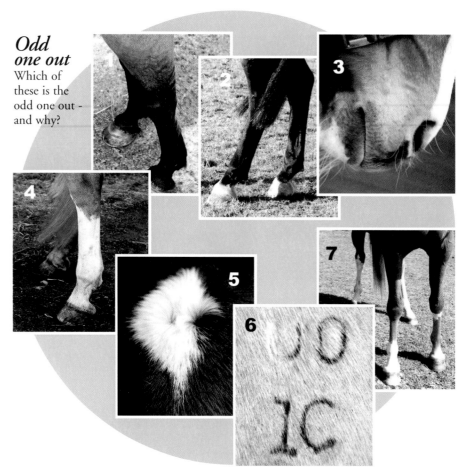

Let me out!

Blaze wants to go out in the field with his companions. Can you tell which path he needs to take?

Grooming by Dan D Brush

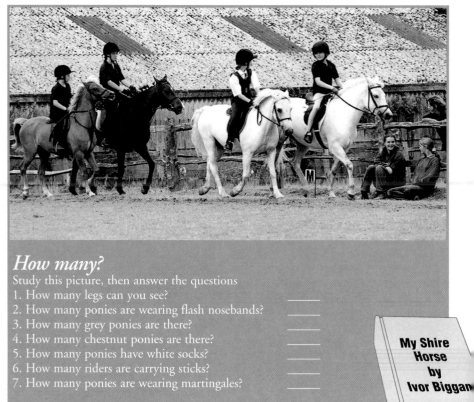

How many?

Study this picture, then answer the questions
1. How many legs can you see?
2. How many ponies are wearing flash nosebands?
3. How many grey ponies are there?
4. How many chestnut ponies are there?
5. How many ponies have white socks?
6. How many riders are carrying sticks?
7. How many ponies are wearing martingales?

My Shire Horse by Ivor Biggan

Colour wordsearch

Can you find all the horse colours we've hidden in our wordsearch?

Words to find

CREAM   GREY   IRON GREY
CHESTNUT   PALOMINO   BAY
SKEWBALD   PIEBALD   DUN

```
j n j o p l j o u k e d t
n c h e s t n u t e a h i
e i h p l e b i a n s t m
p r p i e b a l d o r i s
u o p o w n y p v t l m t
o n o b l h f m u l c s o
c g b l u e r o a n g t c
l r e a s r s t r k r r r
e e l c a e h r a s e e e
g y s k e w b a l d y b a
i u a y e d r d m c e o m
n o o d l y o u i i g r e
l p a l o m i n o n l m d
```

How many words can you make from the words
SHOW JUMPING?

Horsy laughs

What do you call a pony with a sore throat?
A little hoarse!

What do you give a sick horse?
Cough Stirrup!

Why can't horses dance?
Because they have two left feet!

40 Mile Ride by Major Bumsore

Missing words

Read our story, then see if you can fill in the gaps with the words we've provided. But beware - we've added a few bogus words to confuse you. When you've finished, you should have four spare words!

A clear round

Holly was very excited. She was going to her first show 1._ _ _ _ _ _ _ competition with her pony, Sam. Sam was a beautiful grey 2._ _ _ _ _ Mountain pony. Holly had spent the previous day giving Sam a bath and 3._ _ _ _ _ _ _ _ his mane and tail. He looked fantastic. On the morning of the show, Holly could hardly eat her 4._ _ _ _ _ _ _ _ _ . At last it was time to go. With Sam in the 5._ _ _ _ _ _ _ , and Holly in the car with her mother and all the tack, they made their way to the showground.

Once the trailer was parked, Holly went to the secretary's tent to collect her 6._ _ _ _ _ _ . It was 53. When she got back to the trailer, her mother had unloaded Sam and was taking off his travelling boots. Sam was spotless! Holly quickly got dressed and put her riding 7._ _ _ on. As her mother held Sam, Holly mounted, and went to the collecting ring to warm up. There were lots of other riders there, all taking their ponies over the practice 8._ _ _ _ . Sam felt really keen under her. Holly had trouble holding him.

"Steady Sam," she whispered, holding him with her 9._ _ _ _ _ and stroking he grey neck, "we'll be in the ring soon enough."
Sure enough, in no time at all it was Holly's turn to jump.

"Number 53." boomed the loudspeaker. Holly and Sam entered the show ring. Holly could feel her 10._ _ _ _ _ thumping in her chest, and she knew Sam was nervous, too. "Come on Sam," Holly whispered, "we can do it!"

The first jump was a easy rustic to get them going. Sam sailed over. Holly could feel herself grinning - this was going to be fun! The next few jumps seemed like a blur - Sam just jumped them with a 11._ _ _ _ _ of his tail. It was as though he was having a good time. Then they turned to an oxer. The jump seemed much bigger than any of the others.

"Steady Sam, take a good look at this one," Holly said. She needn't have worried, her pony leapt over the jump, giving a little 12._ _ _ _ _ _ as he landed. Then they were over the next jump, and the next, until they flew through the finish - a 13._ _ _ _ _ round!

"Well done Holly!" Holly could hear her mum in the crowd. Leaning down, she 14._ _ _ _ _ _ her wonderful pony. They were in the jump off!

Words

squeal clear patted lunch jumping plaiting whip breakfast trailer swish reins bridle heart jump Welsh number hat Scottish

To discover the solutions to our puzzles, turn to page 94!

The Shetland Pony

The unmistakable Shetland pony is the smallest of Britain's native ponies. Find out all about this tiny pony with a great history and a big heart.

History

It is thought that the Shetland pony existed as long ago as the Bronze Age. The Shetland Isles, the pony's natural habitat, is north of mainland Scotland, and has a bitterly harsh climate. This, combined with the meagre diet Shetland offers the ponies, made sure the breed stayed small in order to survive.

Shetland character

The Shetland pony may be small, but he is courageous and very strong. He can carry more weight, in proportion to his size, than any other horse or pony - he can carry a grown man easily. Quick-witted and intelligent, the Shetland pony is not always a good mount for a child, but when firmly handled, they make willing and talented riding ponies.

Other work

Because of their size, the Shetland pony has always been popular in the circus. They make good pets on a small acreage, and excel as hard-working driving ponies. During the 19th century, black Shetlands were bred for working in the mines, especially when an Act of Parliament banned women and children from working underground.

A popular export

Shetland ponies are in demand all over the world. In the USA they have been crossed with high-stepping Hackney ponies to produce the American Shetland - a much longer-legged breed. Crossed with Appaloosa horses, they have produced the *Pony of the Americas*, and they were foundation stock for the miniature horse - the Falabella.

How to spot a Shetland

Originated from: The Shetland Isles of Scotland.
Colours: Black, grey, chestnut, brown - skewbald and piebald are also allowed, which is unusual for native ponies!
Height: Average of only 10hh. Shetlands are usually measured in centimetres.
How to spot a Shetland: They're small, they're stocky and tough, with thick manes and tails, and short legs. Shetlands have wide nostrils to enable them to warm the cold Shetland air before it enters their body!
Good at: Riding and driving. Their cheeky nature makes them ideal for circus work, and they have a sense of humour, so watch out!
Is a Shetland for you? A Shetland pony has not only great strength, but an abundance of character and a will of his own. If you want to get your own way all the time, don't get a Shetland. These courageous ponies will try their hooves at anything - but you'd better make sure your fencing is low to the ground!

Shetland Pony Factoid
Shetland ponies who live on the Shetland Isles often eat seaweed to supplement their diet!

Shetland Pony Factoid
The ponies who live on the Shetland Isles often carry cut peat for their croft farmers. They also carry seaweed to fertilise the fields.

A visit from the farrier!

In the wild, horses' hooves grow as fast as they wear down, so there is no need to fit protective shoes. However, when we ride horses on the roads, their hooves wear down at a faster rate than they can grow. This is why horses and ponies need shoes!

Specialised job

Horseshoes are made from iron. This tough metal protects hooves from the hard surface of the road. However, as iron is such a hard metal, it has to be heated before it can be shaped into horseshoes. Luckily, the hooves of horses are like our fingernails - you can cut them without hurting the horse, and nail on shoes without them feeling anything. Nevertheless, there are certain areas in the hoof which are very sensitive, so shoeing horses is a very specialised job, indeed.

Mobile shoe shop

Years ago, there used to be a blacksmith in every village. He would not only make horseshoes, but fashion gates and other items out of iron. Today, most farriers operate from a van - they drive from stable to stable, shoeing lots of horses and ponies, and there are so many horses to shoe, they don't get time to make anything else. This means that horses don't have to walk anywhere to get new shoes! This farrier's van has everything in it needed to shoe horses - it's a mobile shoe shop for horses!

Did you know?
Farriers have to serve an apprenticeship for over four years before they are qualified to shoe horses by themselves!

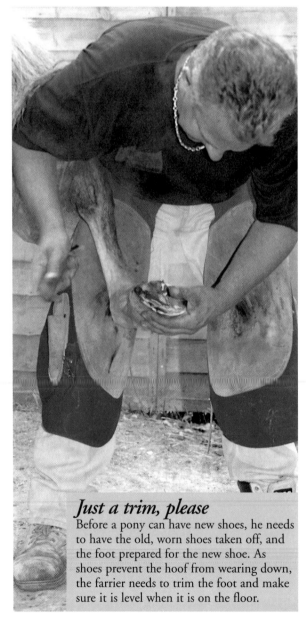

Just a trim, please

Before a pony can have new shoes, he needs to have the old, worn shoes taken off, and the foot prepared for the new shoe. As shoes prevent the hoof from wearing down, the farrier needs to trim the foot and make sure it is level when it is on the floor.

Rasping

The apprentice rasps a hoof down on a different pony. They often work on more than one pony at a time!

Feel the heat

The farrier heats up the shoe and shapes it on the anvil. You can see how hot the shoe is - red hot!

Cool it - nail it!

Once the shoe has cooled down (the farrier puts it in a bucket of water to cool it down quicker) the shoe can be nailed onto the foot. This is where the farrier has to be very careful - the nail must go in the right part of the hoof. The nails, called clenches, are driven through the hoof wall, and the farrier twists them round to cut and finish them off so that they don't stick out. Just another three to go!

Smoking!

With the shoe still hot, the farrier puts it on the pony's hoof to check the shape. As the shoe burns the very edge of the hoof, he can see where he needs to adjust the shoe to fit the foot. Don't worry! Because the hoof is tough, the pony doesn't feel anything - even though there is lots of smoke, and everyone can smell burning!

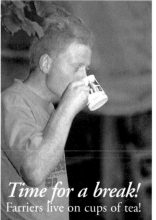

Time for a break!

Farriers live on cups of tea!

Regular service

Shoes can last a horse or pony up to eight weeks - but even if they haven't worn down, they still need to be removed so that the farrier can trim the hooves and keep them in good shape.

With new shoes Olivia and Sunny can go for a ride!

Test yourself!

Test yourself on the pages you have read so far. How many of our questions, based on pages 8 to 25, can you answer? If you write your answers in pencil, you'll be able to rub them out and do the quiz again and again!

1. Can you fill in the points pictured here?

2. How much of his bodyweight does a pony carry on his front legs?

3. True or false?
The hoofpick should be used in the direction of toe to heel.

☐ True ☐ False

4. Which native pony can be black, grey, chestnut, brown, skewbald and piebald?

5. Which way should you hang up a horseshoe for good luck?

6. Thinking about your riding position in the saddle, which of the following statements are right, and which are wrong?

a) Sit tall ☐ right ☐ wrong
b) Lean forward ☐ right ☐ wrong
c) Rest your hands on the saddle ☐ right ☐ wrong
d) Look up and ahead ☐ right ☐ wrong
e) Allow your legs to hang close to your pony's sides ☐ right ☐ wrong
f) Look at your toes ☐ right ☐ wrong
g) Have equal weight on both seat bones ☐ right ☐ wrong
h) Push your heel right down ☐ right ☐ wrong

7. Which breed of horse has a dished face, wide forehead, large nostrils and a high tail carriage?

8. Why do racehorse trainers like a Thoroughbred with a long-striding walk?

9. What is this called, and which grooming brush is it designed to be used with?

10. Name three materials bits can be made from.

1. _____

2. _____

3. _____

11. Why have Shetland ponies got such large nostrils?

_____
_____
_____

12. True or false?
Ponies need their hooves trimmed every three months.
☐ True ☐ False

13. How many beats to a walk stride?

_____

14. Where did the Bedouin tribes keep their Arab horses?

_____

15. What does a Loriner make?

_____

16. Which native pony may eat seaweed in its natural habitat?

_____

17. Why do horses and ponies need to wear shoes?

_____
_____
_____

18. True or false?
A long-striding walk on a long rein is known as a collected walk.
☐ True ☐ False

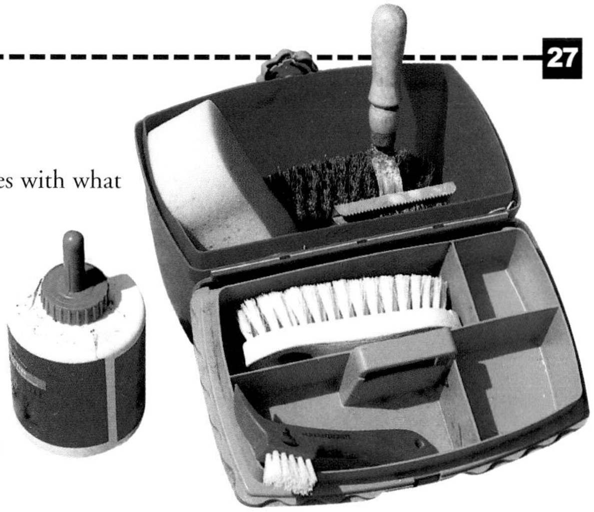

19. Match these grooming brushes with what they are used for
a) Dandy brush
b) Body brush
c) Sponge
d) Water brush

e) Brushing manes and tails
f) Laying the mane
g) Brushing away mud and sweat
h) Cleaning eyes and noses

_____
_____
_____
_____

20. What are clenches?

_____

21. Can you name three different bits?

1. _____

2. _____

3. _____

22. True or false?
The Arabian horse has fewer ribs and tail bones than other horses.
☐ True ☐ False

23. How long does it take to train as a farrier?

_____

24. Which grooming brush shouldn't be used on a pony living out?

_____

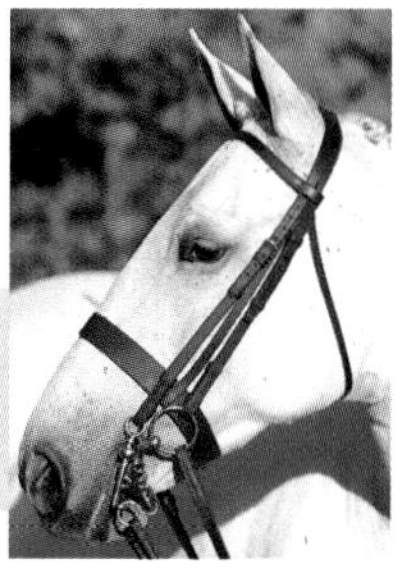

25. Which bridle has two separate bits?

_____

**Turn to page 96 to discover the answers.
Why not see how many times you do the quiz until you get every answer right!**

The trot

Let's look at the trot - a bumpy ride for some!

Two beats

The trot is a pace of two-time. Now, as ponies have four legs this must mean that two legs are on the ground at one time, making a single beat. This is exactly what happens! The trot is a diagonal pace which means that if you think of a pony as having four corners, the two legs on opposite corners work together. So, say the near fore and off hind hit the ground making the first beat of the stride, the pony then springs onto the off fore and near hind to make the second beat. This sounds complicated, but is quite easy if you look at the pictures! So when you trot you should hear two distinct beats - one-two, one-two.

Bouncy!

Because the pony springs from one diagonal pair of legs to the other, the trot is a bouncy, springy pace. It can be difficult to learn to trot because of this. It also feels much faster than walking - and it often is!

Aids to trot

From walk, the rider shortens the reins and closes their legs around their pony until the pony trots. Ponies shorten their necks as they go from walk to trot so shortening the reins ensures the rider has control when the pony changes pace.

Sitting or rising?

Riders can choose to sit to the trot (sitting trot) or they can rise in the stirrups on one diagonal, and sit on the other (rising trot). Rising trot is more comfortable for both horse and rider!

Did you know?
Some horses pace instead of trotting. This means that instead of their diagonal legs making the beats, the legs on each side move together. Pacers are raced in harness - they can go really fast!

Sitting

To sit to the trot, the rider needs to relax - but at the same time, keep their position in the saddle. This is quite difficult, although it is made easier if the horse trots slowly. Western horses are ridden at sitting trot, but they trot so slowly, it is called a jog.

Rising

To rise to the trot, the rider pushes their hips towards their hands and comes out of the saddle. It is important not to pull on the reins to help them rise, and they need to keep their legs in the correct position to help them balance. Our rider in our pictures is rising to the trot. You can see that as one set of legs is on the ground she is sitting, as the other set of legs is on the ground, the rider is rising.

All change!

When riding in a school or manège, it is important to vary which diagonal you rise on - otherwise you are always sitting on the same pair of legs, and wearing them out! For this reason, riders always sit on the outside diagonal - when the outside foreleg is on the ground. So, when they change the rein and go around in the other direction, they change their diagonal by sitting for one beat of the stride.

Why don't you?
When you ride see if you can tell which diagonal you are on by looking at your pony's shoulders. Your pony's foot is on the ground when his shoulder comes towards you. As it goes away from you, he is striding out with that leg, so it is off the ground.

Did you know?
The most collected trot of all is the *piaffe*. This is where a horse will trot on the spot. Highly trained dressage horses are required to perform piaffe in competition - it looks very bouncy for the rider!

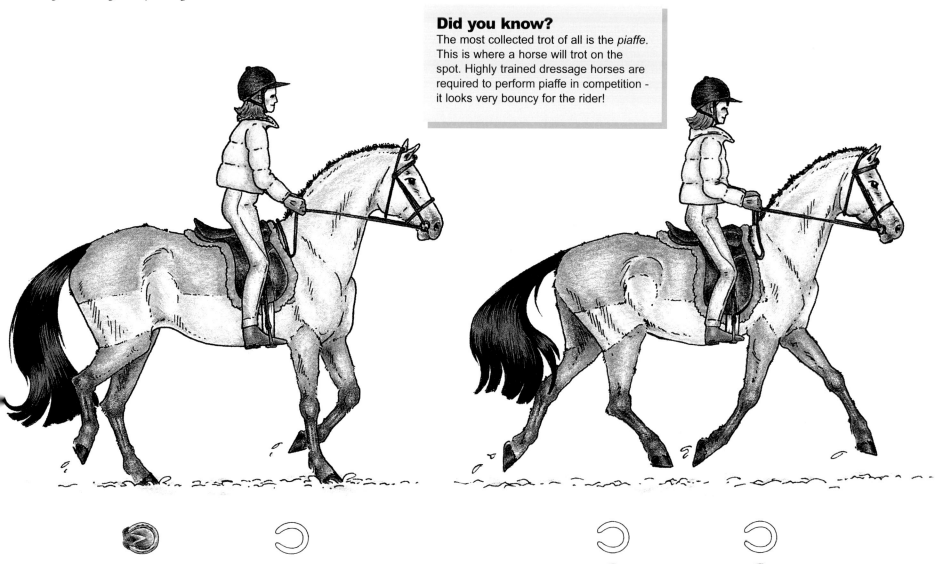

The Shire

If you are looking for an equine record-breaker, here he is! The Shire is the world's tallest and heaviest horse.

History

This massive horse originated from the English shires of Leicestershire, Staffordshire, Derbyshire and Lincolnshire. The Shire is descended from the English Great Horse - King John imported 100 great horses from the Netherlands to breed with English stock to produce large horses for his knights. Later, Dutch workers brought over even more large horses to work the land. These horses became known as the English Black - no doubt because many black Friesian horses influenced the colour.

Knights of old

A medieval knight, kitted out in his heavy armour, could weigh up to 180kg! It needed a special weight-carrying horse to carry him into battle. Imagine the thrilling and terrifying sight these horses and their riders would make, thundering along - would you like to be their enemy?

Ground force

The Shire was put to work on the land. Ploughing, pulling carts and farm machinery, and harnessed to the large drays in the town, the Shire is the gentle giant of the horse world. Famous for its gentle nature, and great strength, he has helped build industry and agriculture.

Saved!

After the second world war, demand for working horses declined. Machinery and motorised transport took over. By the 1960's, under 2000 Shires were recorded in England. Shire enthusiasts were determined that their favourite horses would not become extinct. They organised show classes for Shires at fairs and shows, gave displays, and revised the old skills by giving ploughing demonstrations and organised competitions.

Nowadays, you are likely to see magnificent Shire horses pulling brewer's drays through our city streets, as well as watching their skills at ploughing matches in the country. See if you can see some at shows during the summer months.

Shire Factoid

The world's tallest horse was a Shire named Mammoth. He was measured at 21.2hh!

Shire Factoid

The average weight of a Shire is a tonne!

Shire Factoid

Shires have long hair from the knee to the hooves. This feather protects the legs from the mud when ploughing. It's like a wellington boot! When Shire handlers bath their horses for shows, they dry off the feathering with sawdust.

How to spot a Shire

Originated in: The shires of England.
Colours: Black, grey brown and bay with white feathering (long hair on the legs).
How to spot a Shire: They're big! Bigger than big, they're huge. Standing on average over 17hh, they dwarf their handlers. They've got big feet, too! Heavy in the body, with thick legs and a long neck, the head houses a kindly expression. Everything about the Shire is muscular and powerful. He's built like a tank!
Is a Shire for you? Not unless you've got a farm to plough up, or a huge dray to pull along. Although you can ride a Shire, they're not exactly the ideal mount to turn up with at Pony Club Camp!

A pony of your own!

Owning a pony is great fun - but it's also hard work. This is what makes owning a pony so special - Jessica does everything for her pony, Tyson, and they enjoy a very special relationship because of it.

No days off!

Ponies are very demanding! They need to be cared for every single day, even if they live in a field. They can't just nip down to the supermarket for a snack! If you own a pony you need to be able to visit him every morning and evening, to check he is healthy, to ensure he has clean water and is getting enough to eat, and to be certain that his every need is met. It's up to you to keep him happy, even when it is raining or snowing!

Of course, you may want to go on holiday, or you may even be ill from time to time, so you need to arrange for someone to look after your pony if this happens. There are livery yards which keep horses and ponies for their owners - you may be able to ask one of the staff to help you.

Regular care

You need to feed your own pony, and take care of him. Ponies love routine, they enjoy doing the same things at the same time of day, so you need to keep this in mind when you decide what to do, and when. Here is a list of daily chores your pony will need you to do for him if he is kept in a stable at night.

Daily chores

- Give him feed and clean water
- Groom him
- Turn him out in the field during the day
- Check the water in the field
- Bring him in again at night
- Muck out his stable - and keep it clean
- Ride him
- Clean his tack

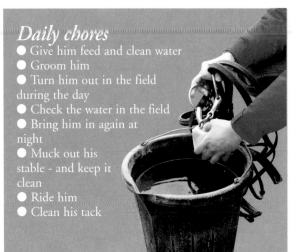

Weekly chores

- Check the field for poisonous plants, and make sure the fencing is sound
- Check his feeding and bedding supplies - and order more if you need them
- Clean your grooming kit
- Check his rugs and tack for repairs

Six-weekly chores

- Get your pony shod
- Give him a worming dose
- Check that his tack still fits him well
- Check his weight - is he gaining or losing weight?

Yearly chores

- Have a vet check him over
- Book his vaccinations

And all this is not taking into account your riding lessons, Pony Club rallies, going to shows and events, and activities which may be organised in your area. Phew!

Did you know?

Lots of mums and dads get hooked on horses and ponies when their children ride. If your parents aren't horsy yet, don't give up hope!

The stable

Your pony's stable needs a thick bed - woodshavings, straw or shredded paper, which needs to be mucked out every day. The bed keeps your pony warm, and saves him standing on a cold, hard floor. Think about giving him a salt or mineral lick in his stable, so that he can help himself when he needs them. Remember that ponies are outdoor animals, and thrive on fresh air. Even though it may be very cold and wet outside, always leave your pony's top stable door open, to let plenty of fresh air in. If you think your pony is cold, then put a rug on him!

Equipment

Ponies need lots of equipment - saddle, bridle, headcollar, rugs, mucking out tools, grooming kit, buckets, mangers, feed bins, tack cleaning equipment. You also need somewhere to put it all!

The field

Fields for ponies need to be well fenced - post and rail is the best. If your pony lives out all the time, make sure he has other horses or ponies for company, and that the field has a good water supply and no poisonous plants. If your field is near a road, ensure the gate is securely fastened, and even padlocked.

Did you know?

Keeping a pony can work out very expensive. You can share a pony with someone, or have someone else's pony on loan for a while, if having your own pony is out of the question.

Daily routine

This is a typical Saturday Jessica has planned for her pony, Tyson.

8.00 am Change Tyson's water and feed him breakfast.
8.15 am Tie Tyson outside his stable and muck out.
8.45 am Tidy the muck heap with Hilary and Emma.
9.30 am Groom Tyson.
10.00 am School Tyson for half-an-hour. Concentrate on transitions, halts and turns.
10.30 am Rub Tyson over and leave him in peace with a haynet. Tidy the yard with Emma and the yard staff.
11.00 am Tidy up Tyson's feed room. Check on supplies.
12.00 am Feed Tyson his lunch. Go for lunch myself!
02.00 pm Saddle Tyson for a hack with Hilary and Jason. Go to the woods and the park.
03.30 pm Rub Tyson down, pick out his feet and leave him with a haynet.
03.45 pm Clean tack.
04.30 pm Tidy Tyson's stable, change his water.
05.00 pm Feed Tyson his dinner and give him his big haynet.
05.45 pm Say goodbye - see him tomorrow!

Why don't you?

If you don't own your own pony, why not see whether anyone at your riding school who does have one, would like you to help them? Remember, they will want go on holiday - they may be grateful for the help!

Saddles

Saddles help the rider to be comfortable when riding - not to mention helping the horse! Read on to discover more about saddles.

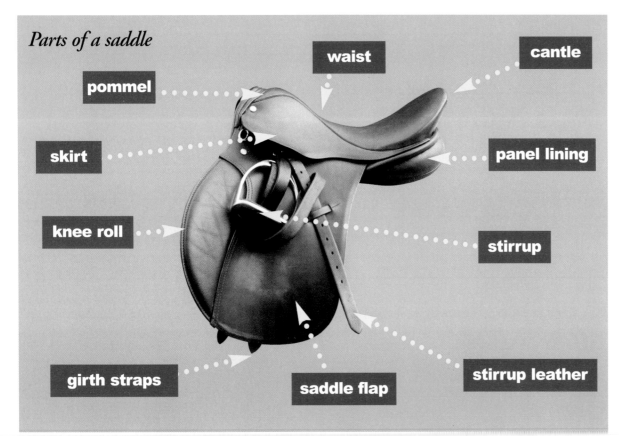

Parts of a saddle

pommel · skirt · knee roll · girth straps · waist · cantle · panel lining · stirrup · saddle flap · stirrup leather

Fitting a saddle

It is very important to fit a saddle correctly to each individual horse or pony. The saddle is built on a tree which allows space for the spine. The weight of the rider is taken on either side of the spine and there must be plenty of clearance at the front where the wither is. Of course, there must be no weight on the spine when the weight of the rider is actually in the saddle, so the saddle needs to be fitted with the rider on board. You should be able to see daylight all the way through the middle - just as you can here in this photograph.

General purpose

For most people, a general purpose saddle does the job as it is somewhere between the extremes of a jumping and a dressage saddle.

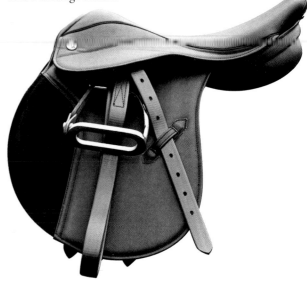

The jumping saddle

Show jumpers ride with short stirrups, so that they can get up and out of the saddle over the jumps. The flap of a showjumping saddle is built further forward for this reason.

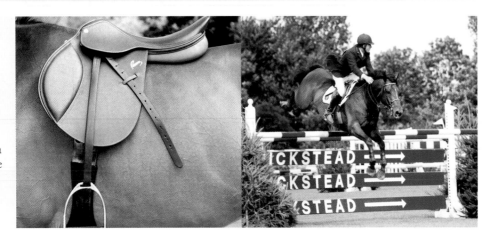

Dressage saddle

Dressage riders ride with very long stirrups - they need to use their legs to let their horses know what to do, and sit deep in the saddle. The dressage saddle has long, straight panels. You can also see that the girth is fastened below the saddle flap, rather than underneath it. This allows the rider to get their leg really close to the horse.

Did you know?

Horses and ponies can change shape throughout the year, especially if they are growing, or are out at grass and their weight changed with the seasons. Saddles need to be checked to ensure they fit - they may need to be altered as the horse changes shape.

Did you know?

There are now saddles with special air panels which are more comfortable for the horse, and do not go lumpy like stuffed panels can do.

Western saddle

This specialist saddle has a horn at the front to enable the rider to rope a cow - the rope goes around the horn! The tooled leather is very fancy, the stirrups are covered in leather, and the horse wears a blanket under the saddle. You can see a hole where a second girth - called a cinch - can be fitted. This is essential if the horse is used for roping cattle, as the strain on the horn can pull the saddle off over his neck!

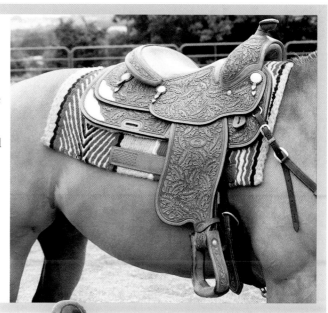

Racing saddles

Racehorses need to have saddles which do not weigh much - so racing saddles are tiny, with light stirrups. Do you think you would be comfortable in a racing saddle?

Did you know?

You can get special covers to keep your saddle clean and dry.

Side saddle

Ladies who want to ride side saddle need a special saddle with two pommels on the near side. Their left leg goes under the lower pommel, their right leg hooks over the upper pommel. Side saddles need a second girth to help them stay balanced on the horse. From the back, it should look as though the lady is sitting astride, but with her right leg missing - not all lopsided! Riding side saddle is very elegant and the ladies have to wear a veil under their top hats, and wear their hair in a bun!

Why don't you?

Check out the saddles at your riding school or local show. See how many different ones you can see - and the different colours you can spot. You'll be amazed at the variety!

Colour magic!

There are many different horse and pony colours. Even though the main colours are shown here, there are lots of different variations and shades - so you may see a horse or pony which looks different to the ones pictured!

white (pink eyes and skin)

iron grey

Things to look for

Points

It is not just body colour which determines a horse's colour. A bay horse has a brown or chestnut body, with black points. Points are mane and tail, legs and tips of the ears.

Hooves

When looking at horse colours, check the hooves. Horses with pale legs often have pale hooves - dark legged horses will have black hooves.

Muzzle

Look at the muzzle, too. A brown horse may look black, but will have a pale muzzle and underbelly. A grey horse will have a darker muzzle and black skin, but a pure white horse will have pink skin and even pink eyes. White horses are very rare!

Specialists

Certain breeds of horses and ponies may be a specific colour. For example, Exmoor ponies are always brown with pale muzzles, rings around their eyes, and a pale underbelly. This is a very ancient colour. Fjord ponies are a traditional dun colouring, and the Austrian Haflinger is always chestnut.

black

appaloosa

tri-coloured

brown

chestnut

liver chestnut

bright bay

dark bay

dapple grey

flea-bitten grey

cream
(blue eyes)

rose grey

skewbald

dun

palomino

piebald

chestnut
(flaxen mane
and tail)

strawberry
roan

bay roan

blue roan

The Horses of Iberia

The Iberian Peninsula comprises Spain and Portugal. The horses of Iberia have Barb and Arabian ancestry. However, for centuries the breeds have been kept pure, and have also been used to improve many European horse breeds.

The two main breeds

There are two main breeds in Iberia - the Spanish Horse, which used to be known as the Andalucian, and the Lusitano from Portugal. Portugal used to be known as Lusitania, which explains where the breed gets its name! The ancient Romans appreciated both breeds, and many horse breeding farms were set up in the Roman Empire to breed war horses, as well as those which excelled at chariot racing. You can imagine these noble horses racing in the arena, necks stretched, their manes flowing, the roar of the crowd in their ears as they galloped to glory.

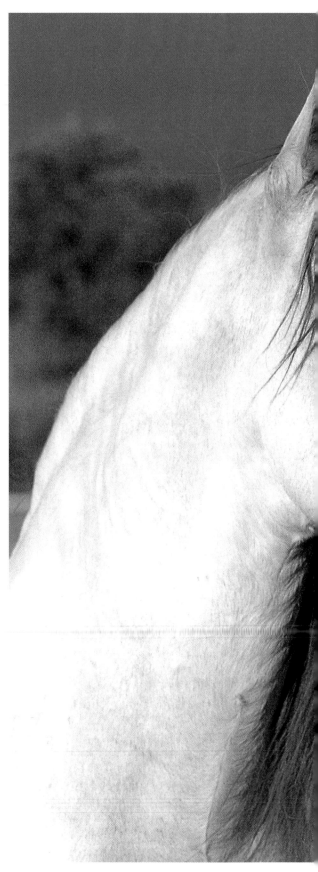

Spanish Horse Factoid

Traditionally, the manes and tails of the mare are hogged and docked. Only the stallions are allowed the luxury of their manes and tails!

The Spanish Horse

Usually grey or bay, this majestic horse stands about 15.2hh. With a high knee action characteristic of the breed, the Spanish Horse is an impressive sight, especially when wearing traditional saddlery and a costumed rider. *Jerez de la Frontera* is famous for making sherry, hosting an annual fair or *feria*, and is home to the Royal Riding School of Spain. Public performances are given weekly, so if you are ever lucky enough to visit this part of Spain, make a date to see the dancing horses as they perform classical equitation for the appreciative crowds.

The Lusitano

The native breed of Portugal - they are the same size as the Spanish Horse, although a little finer in build. The ancient Romans prized this horse so much that they concentrated their horse breeding and sport in Portugal when they ruled there over 2000 years ago. The Lusitano excels in the bullring (in Portugal, the bull is not killed), and is also brilliant at high school work.

Lusitano Factoid

Agile and intelligent, the Lusitano is ideal for helping their riders tend the herds of fighting bulls.

Alter-Real

The Alter-Real was bred to perform *Haute École*, high school dressage. They originated from 300 Spanish mares brought to *Alter do Chão*, a Portuguese province of Alentejo in 1748. *Real* is Portuguese for royal - the horses were bred for the royal stables in Lisbon. Like all Iberian horses, the Alter-Real is built for classical equitation, and they perform at the *Escola Portuguesa D'arte Equestre* - the Portuguese School of Equestrian Art. Wearing traditional costumes and saddlery from the 18th century, they make a splendid spectacle, as you can see below!

Iberian breed factoid

Both the Spanish Horse and the Lusitano share the characteristics of fine, wavy manes and tails. They are famous for their kind and gentle temperament.

The canter

Everyone loves cantering!

Footfalls

As a pony pushes off into canter the outside hind leg begins the stride. In our drawing, this is the near hind leg. The next beat is made from the off hind leg and the near fore leg coming down together to make a single beat. The next and last beat of the stride is made by the off fore leg. This is the leading leg. You can see quite clearly in the picture that the legs nearest us are taking longer strides than the legs farthest away. This means that the horse will be going circling to the right.

Three beats

The canter has three beats to every stride. This must mean that two hooves are on the ground at the same time, making a single beat. The beat is one-two-three... one-two-three.

Legs, legs, legs

When a pony canters, the way its legs work depends on which direction it is circling. The legs on one side take a longer stride than on the other side. This means that, when the pony canters in a circle, it is important that the legs taking a longer stride are on the inside. If they were on the outside, they could cross over and cause a problem! The foreleg which takes the longer stride is called the *leading* leg.

Did you know?

The sequence of footfalls we have looked at doesn't always happen - although they should be like that. Sometimes, horses and ponies canter *disunited*, and this means that their front two legs have a leading leg on one side, whilst the back two legs have the opposite leg leading. This is very uncomfortable!

A moment of suspension

As the pony completes its stride, there is a moment when all four legs are off the ground - and then the sequence begins again. This is called a *moment of suspension* and it gives the canter its lovely rocking-horse action which is so comfortable. In trot, the pony's back springs about in a bouncy way, but in canter, the action is far more rolling. So, although cantering can be faster than trotting, it can be much more comfortable!

Aids to canter

Asking a pony to canter isn't just a question of getting it to go faster! Remember, you are asking your pony to change what his legs are doing, so you need to be quite clear with your aids. If you rise to the trot and use your legs, your pony will probably just trot faster! So, instead, this is what you need to do:

● Stop rising. As you ask for canter, sit to the trot.
● Ask for a slight bend by feeling on your inside rein.
● Use your outside leg behind the girth - this tells your pony you want him to start cantering on that leg.
● Use your inside leg on the girth - this tells your pony to go!

What to do

When cantering the rider should sit up tall in the saddle and sit very still, allowing their lower body to move with the pony. Sometimes, when a rider is riding across country, or cantering for a long time, they may stand up in the stirrups and adopt what is known as a *forward seat*. This helps to keep the weight off their horse's back.

Why don't you?
You can check which leg your pony is on when you are cantering. Just glance down at his shoulders - one of them will be going forward further than the other. This is the leading leg. Try it!

Horsy makes for you to try!

Have a go at our fabulous horsy makes. Ideal for a rainy day, or for when boredom strikes!

Make a horsy bookmark

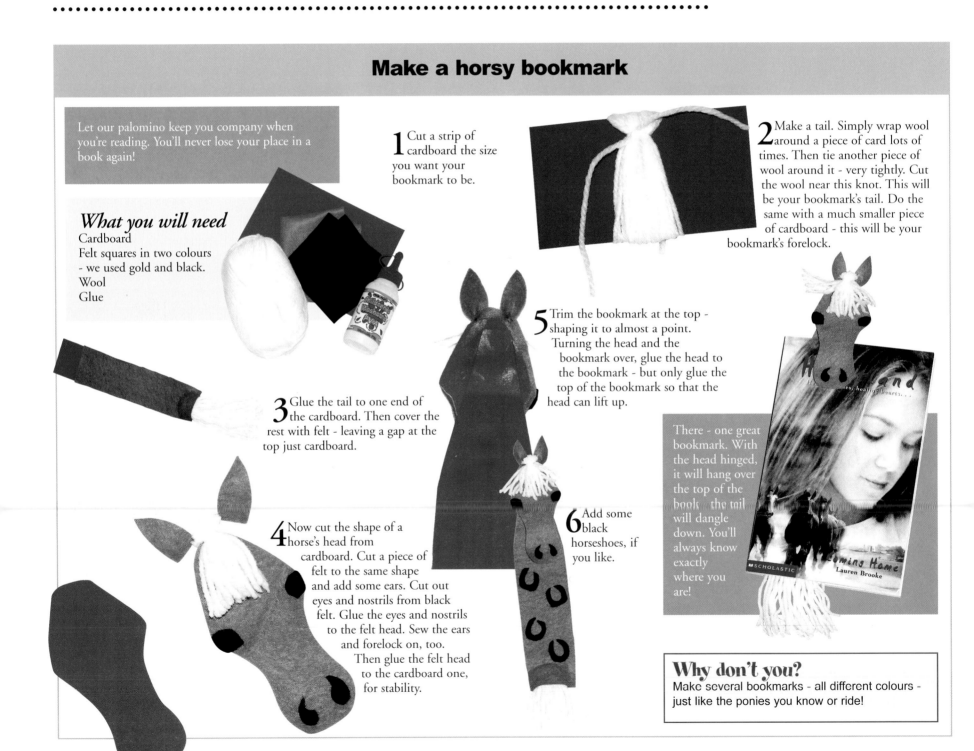

Let our palomino keep you company when you're reading. You'll never lose your place in a book again!

What you will need
Cardboard
Felt squares in two colours - we used gold and black.
Wool
Glue

1 Cut a strip of cardboard the size you want your bookmark to be.

2 Make a tail. Simply wrap wool around a piece of card lots of times. Then tie another piece of wool around it - very tightly. Cut the wool near this knot. This will be your bookmark's tail. Do the same with a much smaller piece of cardboard - this will be your bookmark's forelock.

3 Glue the tail to one end of the cardboard. Then cover the rest with felt - leaving a gap at the top just cardboard.

4 Now cut the shape of a horse's head from cardboard. Cut a piece of felt to the same shape and add some ears. Cut out eyes and nostrils from black felt. Glue the eyes and nostrils to the felt head. Sew the ears and forelock on, too. Then glue the felt head to the cardboard one, for stability.

5 Trim the bookmark at the top - shaping it to almost a point. Turning the head and the bookmark over, glue the head to the bookmark - but only glue the top of the bookmark so that the head can lift up.

6 Add some black horseshoes, if you like.

There - one great bookmark. With the head hinged, it will hang over the top of the book, the tail will dangle down. You'll always know exactly where you are!

Why don't you?
Make several bookmarks - all different colours - just like the ponies you know or ride!

Make a pizza pony

This pizza pony looks so good, we bet you won't want to eat him!

What you will need
Pizza base mix
Tomato puréc
Cheese
Choice of toppings!

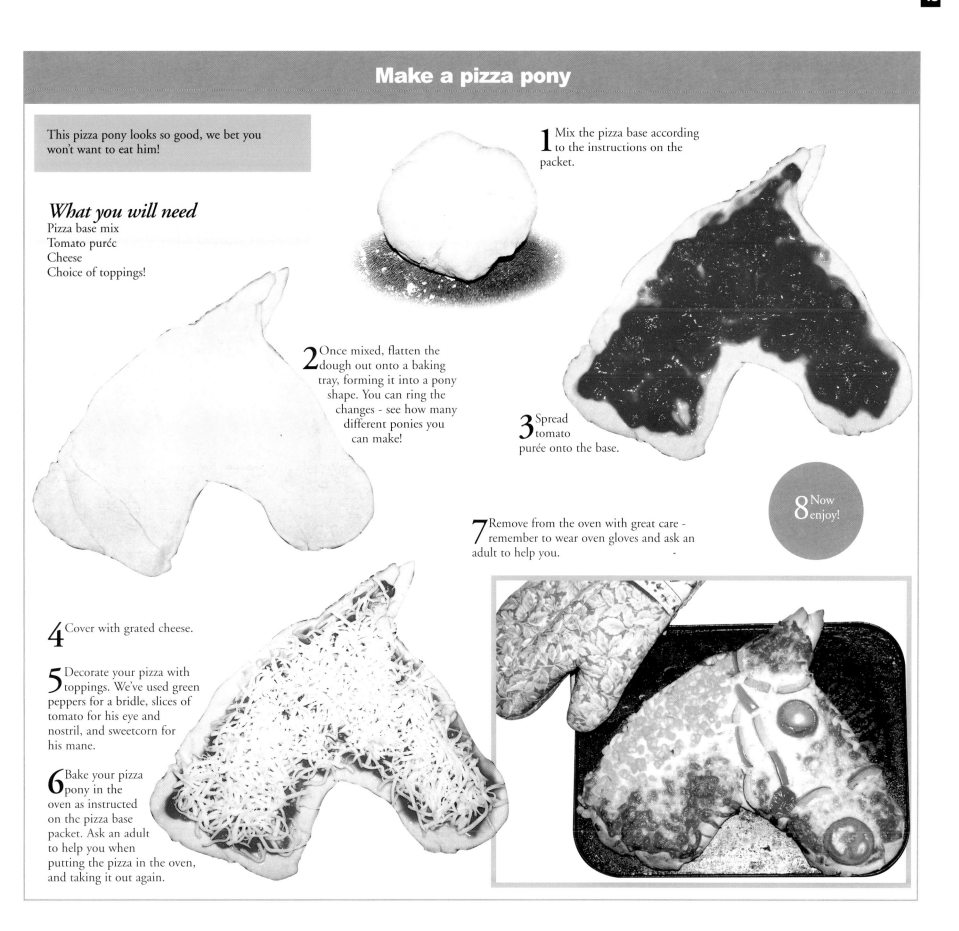

1 Mix the pizza base according to the instructions on the packet.

2 Once mixed, flatten the dough out onto a baking tray, forming it into a pony shape. You can ring the changes - see how many different ponies you can make!

3 Spread tomato purée onto the base.

4 Cover with grated cheese.

5 Decorate your pizza with toppings. We've used green peppers for a bridle, slices of tomato for his eye and nostril, and sweetcorn for his mane.

6 Bake your pizza pony in the oven as instructed on the pizza base packet. Ask an adult to help you when putting the pizza in the oven, and taking it out again.

7 Remove from the oven with great care - remember to wear oven gloves and ask an adult to help you.

8 Now enjoy!

Test yourself!

Test yourself on the pages since the last quiz. How many of our questions, based on pages 28 to 43 can you answer? If you write your answers in pencil, you can rub them out and have another go later on!

5. Which is the best fencing you can have around a pony's field?

_____

_____

6. Which breed of horses did the Ancient Romans prize so highly?

_____

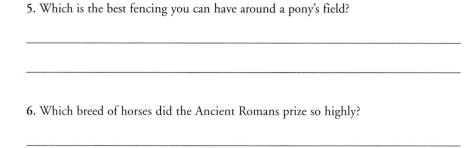

7. What is a western girth called?

_____

8. How do side saddle riders wear their hair?

_____

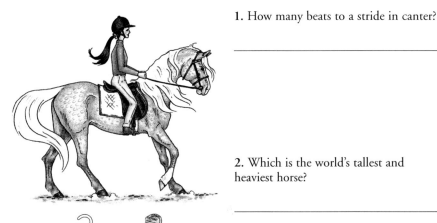

1. How many beats to a stride in canter?

_____

2. Which is the world's tallest and heaviest horse?

_____

_____

9. Name three chores you would need to do for your pony every day.

_____

_____

_____

3. Which of these are correct aids to canter?
a) Sit to the trot ☐ right ☐ wrong
b) Rise to the trot ☐ right ☐ wrong
c) Use the outside leg at the girth ☐ right ☐ wrong
d) Use the inside leg at the girth ☐ right ☐ wrong
e) Use the outside leg behind the girth ☐ right ☐ wrong
f) Use the inside leg behind the girth ☐ right ☐ wrong

4. Can you name the colours of the horses pictured here?

_____

_____

_____

_____

10. When rising to the trot, does the rider sit on the outside diagonal, or the inside diagonal?

_____

11. How many Shires were there in the 1960's?
a) 200 ☐
b) 2,000 ☐
c) 20,000 ☐

12. Which saddle has a straight saddle flap and a girth fastening below the flaps?
a) Show jumping ☐
b) Dressage ☐
c) General Purpose. ☐

13. True or False
Piaffe is a highly collected trot.
☐ True ☐ False

14. What is the average weight of a Shire horse?

_____

15. Name the native horse of Portugal.

_____

16. True or False?
You should always keep the top part of a stable door open because ponies love fresh air.
☐ True ☐ False

17. How should you sit when cantering?

_____

_____

_____

18. Name three different grey colourings in horses.

_____

_____

_____

19. True or False?
Spanish stallions are hogged and docked.
☐ True ☐ False

20. What are points?
a) Colouring of the mane, tail, legs and ears ☐.
b) Parts of a jump ☐.
d) The tips of a pony's hooves ☐.

21. Name these parts of the saddle.

22. What is the Andalucian breed of horse now known as?

_____

23. How many pommels does a side saddle have?

_____

24. Name two types of bedding suitable for a pony's stable.

_____

_____

Turn to page 96 to discover the answers.
See how many times you do the quiz before you get every answer right!

Jumping!

What happens when a pony jumps? Well, there are five distinct stages - and here they are!

Did you know?
Because of where their eyes are positioned on their heads, horses and ponies cannot see directly under their own noses. This means that as they go over a jump, they cannot see it - they jump from memory! This is another reason to get a really good approach to a jump.

Stage one - *the approach*

How a pony approaches the jump is very important, and this is largely up to the rider. The pony needs to be going forward with plenty of energy - but not speed. He needs to be able to see the jump and should meet is straight and in the centre. This gives him the best possible chance of jumping it well. A bad approach will usually result in a poor jump.

Stage three - *the moment of suspension*

As he goes over the jump with all four legs off the ground, the pony should round his back and clear the fence.

Stage four - *the landing*

As the pony prepares to land his head comes up and his forelegs touch down. His back should be supple to allow his hind legs to come under him as they prepare to touch the ground.

Stage two - *the take off*

Just before he takes off, a pony will lower his head and stretch his neck, taking a good look. Then, as he takes off, his neck shortens again, he raises his head and tucks his forelegs up under his chest. His hindquarters propel him forward and upward.

Starting jumping

When you first start jumping you may be able to hold on to a neck strap to help you balance. Jumping is very exciting and you need to be able to fold your upper body forward, without losing your balance. The secret is to keep your legs under you, and your heels well down. Always look up and forward when jumping - and don't forget to breathe in the excitement!

Stage five - *the getaway*

Okay, so the jump is over - but there may be another one ahead! The getaway needs to be flowing and smooth, with the rider in control, looking toward and planning the next fence.

Tacking up!

Before you can go for a ride, you need to be able to tack up your pony!

Putting on a saddle

Check your pony's back before saddling him. You need to look for any lumps and bumps, and anything which may have settled on him since you groomed him.

Put the saddle on, placing it on the pony's neck and sliding it back to the right place. This makes certain all the coat is flat under the saddle, and comfortable.

Go around the other side of your pony and pull down the girth, taking care that it doesn't bang against your pony. Check under the saddle on this side to make sure everything is straight and comfortable.

From the near side, do up the girth. At this stage, do it up so that it is quite loose. How would you like a belt tightened really tightly around your middle all of a sudden?

Pull the buckle guard down. This protects the saddle flap from being rubbed by the girth buckles.

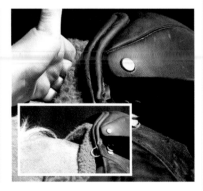

Check that the numnah is pulled right up into the arch of the saddle. This ensures it doesn't put pressure on your pony's spine.

Saddles first

Try to put the saddle on your pony first. This allows your pony's back to get used to the saddle, and for it to warm up - especially in the winter.

Did you know?

The pony's left side is called his near side. His right side is called is off side.

Did you know?

Tack doesn't have to be made of leather - you can get synthetic tack, too!

Putting on a bridle

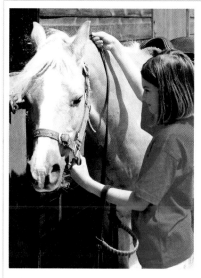

Why don't you?

Watch other people tack up their horses and ponies - you may pick up some handy tips!

Always put the reins on over your pony's neck before anything else. This will prevent them from dangling down around his legs, and it also means you have something to hold him by when you take off his headcollar!

With the headcollar undone, hold the cheekpieces of the bridle over your pony's face (this stops him putting his head up out of reach!), and feed the bit into his mouth. If he won't open up for you, put your thumb in the very corner of his mouth where he has no teeth. This should get him to open up!

Gently put the headpiece over your pony's ears, taking care not to bend them backwards or fold them up, which would be uncomfortable for him.

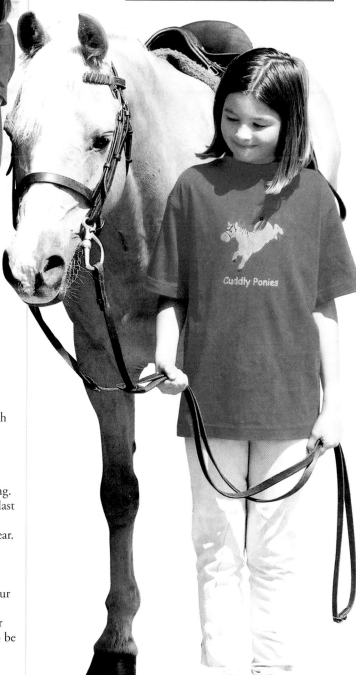

Once the bridle is on, all you need to do is do up the throatlash (not too tightly)...

... and the noseband and curb chain, if you have one.

Remember!
Don't forget to tighten the girth before you get on!

Remember!
Keep your tack clean and shining. Not only will it look smart and last longer, but it will be more comfortable for your pony to wear.

Remember!
Take as much care removing your tack as you did putting it on. Rough handling can hurt your pony, and make him reluctant to be tacked up next time.

There! Your pony is all ready to go for a ride.

Puzzle fun!

Try our horsy puzzles!

Square by square

Can you draw this pony by copying square by square?

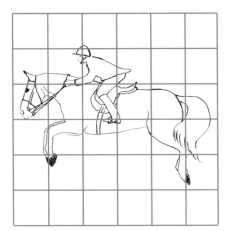

Odd one out

Which of these is the odd one out - and why?

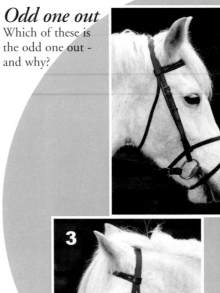

Where's my breakfast?

Dinky is waiting for his breakfast - can you discover which path his owner needs to take to feed him?

**Keeping
Five Ponies
by
Rich Kidd**

How many?

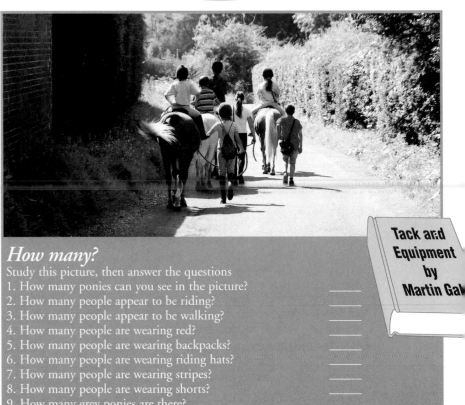

Study this picture, then answer the questions
1. How many ponies can you see in the picture?
2. How many people appear to be riding?
3. How many people appear to be walking?
4. How many people are wearing red?
5. How many people are wearing backpacks?
6. How many people are wearing riding hats?
7. How many people are wearing stripes?
8. How many people are wearing shorts?
9. How many grey ponies are there?

**Tack and
Equipment
by
Martin Gal**

Long Distance Riding by N Durance

Breed wordsearch

Can you find all the breeds we've hidden in our wordsearch?

Words to find

EXMOOR
APPALOOSA
LUSITANO
SHIRE

FJORD
ZEBRA
ARABIAN
SHETLAND

DONKEY
NEW FOREST
LIPIZZANER
MULE

```
j n l o p l j c u k e d a
a o i e x m o o r l a h p
r r p p l j m x a u f t p
a d i n a p e l d s j i a
b e z e b r a e v i o m l
i t z e l d f m u t r s o
a n a t c t i a i a d t o
n e n l s r s r r n s r s
s h e t l a n d a o s e a
g b r t g n e e n k h b a
i u m u l e r t m c i o l
n e w f o r e s t i r r e
l g u y d o n k e y e m d
```

How many words can you make from the words
THREE DAY EVENT?

Horsy laughs

Did you hear about the horse called Tank Top? He was a great jumper!

What do you call a donkey with three legs?
Wonkey Donkey!

A horse went into a shop and the shopkeeper said, *"Why the long face?"*

Missing words

Read our story, then see if you can fill in the gaps with the words we've provided. But watch out! We've added a few bogus words to confuse you. When you have finished, you should have four spare words!

A great hack

It was such a lovely sunny day, Kerry decided to take her pony, Goldie, for a **1.**_ _ _ _ around the farm. Goldie was a beautiful **2.**_ _ _ _ _ _ _ _ pony, the colour of brushed gold with a snowy **3.**_ _ _ _ _ mane and tail. Kerry had owned Goldie for two years - they were a great partnership.

After **4.**_ _ _ _ _ _ _ _ Goldie, Kerry fetched her tack. Goldie always pulled faces when she saddled him up - Kerry just laughed at him. With the bridle on, Kerry fetched her riding **5.**_ _ _ and led her pony to the mounting block.

"Now just stand **6.**_ _ _ _ _ while I get on you," Kerry said. Goldie stood as still as a **7.**_ _ _ _ and Kerry lowered herself gently into his **8.**_ _ _ _ _ _ _. Goldie tossed his head. He was impatient to be off - he loved **9.**_ _ _ _ _ _ _ around the farm.

They set off - with Goldie striding out. Kerry always felt good when she was riding her pony around the **10.**_ _ _ _. With the sun **11.**_ _ _ _ _ _ _ and the birds **12.**_ _ _ _ _ _ _, she felt on top of the world. Leaning forward, Kerry **13.**_ _ _ _ _ _ Goldie's neck.

"This is great, isn't it boy? " she whispered. Goldie **14.**_ _ _ _ _ _ _ _. It was as though he understood what Kerry was saying. He liked going for a ride as much as she did. When they reached the hayfield, Kerry leant **15.**_ _ _ _ _ _ _ _. Goldie sensed her mood - he started to dance underneath her.

"Steady boy," Kerry laughed, "we'll go for a **16.**_ _ _ _ _ _ here!" She only had to lean forward and Goldie was off - galloping like the wind. Kerry leant forward over his neck, the wind drawing tears from her **17.**_ _ _ _. She felt like singing! Gradually, they reached the end of the field and Goldie slowed to a **18.**_ _ _ _. Damp patches of sweat showed on Goldie's neck and Kerry felt **19.**_ _ _ too. "We'll walk home," she said, turning her pony around. It had been a great ride!

Words

hat palomino farm gloves shining cold patted forward wind ride hot gallop walk still grooming white hacking snorted eyes saddle singing rock birds

Turn to page 94 to discover the answers

The Fjord

The Fjord horse is one of the most striking and easily recognised horses in the world. Read on to discover more about this ancient breed.

History

The Fjord Horse looks very much like the Asiatic Wild Horse - just like the ones ancient cave dwellers drew on the walls of their caves. It's colouring and build make it easy to imagine them sharing an ancient world with our ancestors.

Native to Norway, the Fjord Horse was the war horse of the ancient Vikings. This conquering race used to pit their stallions against one another - horse fighting was a popular sport.

What they look like

You can't miss a Fjord Horse! With their characteristic dun colouring, ancient dark dorsal stripe along their spine, and zebra markings on the legs, they look every inch the ancient horse! The most striking feature of the Fjord is its upright mane - hogged to make it stand erect. The centre hair is black, and clever trimming allows it to stand proud of the silver hair either side.

What do they do?

In Norway, the Fjord works as a riding horse, a pack horse, in harness - and is even used for ploughing. It is a hardy breed, which does well on little feed, and is famous for its stamina and courage.

How to spot a Fjord Horse

Originated in: Norway.
Colour: Always light dun with a black and silver mane.
Height: Between 13 - 14hh.
How to spot a Fjord: Easy! They all look exactly the same!
Good at: Great family horses, the strong Fjord will excel at anything - and every member of the family will be able to ride him.
Is a Fjord for you? If you want a hardy pony who likes to turn his hooves to anything you ask, a Fjord is for you. They are becoming more popular in Great Britain, with more being seen at shows and events - so look out for them!

Fjord Horse Factoid
There has been a strict breeding programme for the Fjord Horse in Norway since the beginning of the 20th century.

At the riding school

Choosing a good riding school is very important. How many of the things you should look for can you spot in our picture?

- A good riding school will be approved by the British Horse Society or the Association of British Riding Schools. This means that the horses and ponies are well cared for and the instructors are qualified.
- Lessons are small and well organised - safe and interesting for everyone.
- The yard is well organised, clean and tidy.
- The ponies look well-cared for - bright-eyed and friendly.
- Tack is clean and safe.
- The staff are friendly and make you welcome.
- The office is well organised and lessons graded.
- Tools are all put away tidily, not left lying around.
- The muck heap is tidy and away from the yard.
- Paddocks are well fenced, with clean water troughs.
- There is no dung lying around, or equipment left out.
- Everyone seems to enjoy their lessons!

OFFICE

TACK ROOM

IN CASE OF EMERGENCIES
RELEASE ALL HORSES AND PHONE FIRE BRIGADE (999).
ALSO PHONE CINDY GLEN
0142 850031

FEED ROOM

HORSES NAME	SHORT FEED	HAY

Horsy makes for you to try!

Why not try your hand at our great horsy makes? They're not difficult - so what are you waiting for?

Make a horse calendar

You'll never forget the date with this beautiful horse to remind you.

You will need
A piece of cardboard - we picked this fabulous silver card
A horse poster. Ours came from a horsy magazine
Calendar (available from stationers)
Ribbon
Glue

1 Cut out the poster - this one looks good with no background. Paste this carefully onto the cardboard.

2 Glue the ribbon to the top of the cardboard - remember to stick it to the wrong side. This will enable you to hang the calendar up.

3 Using two pieces of ribbon, sticky tape the calendar to the bottom of the cardboard - again, sticking it to the wrong side.

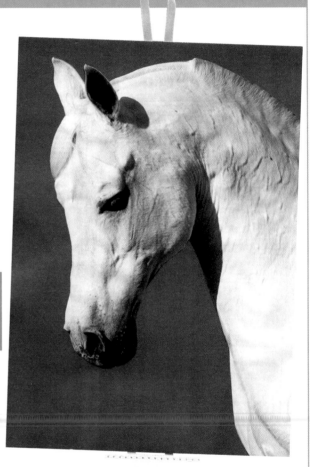

4 Now your calendar is ready to hang up. Doesn't it look great?

Why don't you?
Make a calendar and use a picture of your favourite pet? They make great gifts!

Make a rosette

This two-tone rosette will look cool in your bedroom - or in your pony's stable.

You will need

Ribbon in two colours - one wider than the other.
Cardboard
A picture of your pony
Narrow ribbon
Glue
Needle and thread

1 Cut a circle of cardboard - we used a paper cup to get a perfect circle.

2 Pleating the widest ribbon, sew it carefully to the cardboard.

3 Now sew the narrow ribbon over the first layer. Be sure to start in the same place.

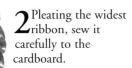

4 Carefully cut out the tails. We've used two narrow tails and one wide tail. Point the ends. Sew them onto the middle of the circle - over the narrow pleated row.

5 Turn the rosette over and fasten a loop of narrow ribbon at the top to hang your rosette up. Cover the back with another circle of cardboard to make it neat.

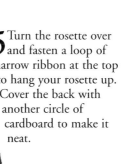

6 Turn the rosette over to its right side. Stick a picture of your favourite pony in the centre. We framed it with a circle cut from silver card - to make it extra special!

Now all you have to do is decide where to hang your fabulous rosette!

The Appaloosa

The Appaloosa is more than just a spotted horse - it is a breed, with its own characteristics and traits which make it unique.

The Appaloosa is a specific breed which was developed by the Nez Percé American Indians in the mid-18th century. The Nez Percé tribes lived near the banks of several rivers, including the Palouse river. It is from this river that the *Ap-Palouse* horse got its name.

History

When the Spanish conquistadors invaded the Americas, they brought with them their own horses as horses were not native to the USA. A number of these horses, left behind by the Spanish, carried spotted genes, and these were passed onto subsequent generations of horses which bred wild. The Nez Percé knew a great deal about breeding horses and they were very fussy about the horses they bred from, ensuring only the very best were allowed to carry on their line. Colour wasn't the only consideration as the Nez Percé needed tough work horses which could carry them in war, and hunt with them, too.

Almost wiped out...

This wonderful breed was almost destroyed when the US government started to confiscate Native American lands and move the people onto reservations. Understandably, the Nez Percé people resisted this move and under their leader, Chief Joseph, fought the cavalry. The tribes marched over 1,300 miles to try to escape to Canada, but they didn't make it and were stopped by the USA solders in Montana, just short of the border. Sadly, the cavalry took all the Nez Percé's possessions and herds of their beautiful horses were slaughtered.

...but not quite

Thankfully, a few of the Appaloosa horses survived, and the breed developed from these saved horses. The Appaloosa Horse Club was formed in Idaho in 1938. Over the next 50 years, over 400,000 Appaloosas were registered - the third largest horse registry in the world. What a success story!

How to spot an Appaloosa

Originated in: The USA.
Colours: There are five main coat patterns, Leopard, Snowflake, Blanket, Marbleized and Frost.
Height: Between 14.2 - 15.2hh.
How to spot an Appaloosa: Spotted coat, thin and sparse mane and tail, white area surrounding the eye, mottled skin on the muzzle, and striped hooves.
Good at: Appaloosas make great riding horses, they can jump and are good at endurance events.
Is an Appaloosa for you? These horses are gentle and kind. They will try to please their riders and will try their hooves at anything! They are also hardy, as well as being very striking to look at. Don't get an Appaloosa if you want to melt into the background!

Appaloosa factoid
Did you know that you can have Appaloosa horses without any spots - but they still breed spotted offspring!

Appaloosa factoid

The six coat patterns are as follows;

Leopard - white coat with dark spots.

Snowflake - dark coat with white spots.

Spotted blanket - dark coat with dark spots on white hindquarters.

Marble - dark coat at birth which fades almost to white.

Frosted - mostly dark with light spots on the loins and hips.

What to wear

Deciding what to wear when riding and around horses and ponies isn't all about looking good - there are safety aspects to take into consideration. Take a look at our suggestions for looking stylish - and staying safe - in and out of the saddle.

Clothes for safety

A riding hat is a must. These are made to a strict standard and carry approval tickets. Look for the latest, safest approval standard for your riding hat, and make sure it fits really well. It should be snug, without being too tight, and the chinstrap needs to fit comfortably so that the hat does not fall off if you do!

Hacking
For hacking, this outfit is ideal.

A *body protector* is a great safety garment. These fit tightly and offer protection should you fall off and your pony treads on you by accident. Like your hat, it needs to fit well, so make sure you get it fitted when you buy it. Body protectors are approved to a standard too, and they are available in several different levels. Make sure yours is right for you.

Riding clothes should *fit you well* - not flap about in the breeze and scare your pony. Wear long sleeves, too. These will protect you from branches and bushes if you ride out in the woods. Whatever you wear, make sure you can move about easily in it - no tight tops and uncomfortable underwear!

Gloves are a must. They prevent your reins from slipping through your fingers and are great when it's cold and wet, too!

Jodhpurs are the most comfortable legwear of all - they are designed for the job! Stretchy and reinforced in all the right places, they come in some really snazzy colours, as well as traditional beige.

Half chaps are designed to fit over short boots and jodhpurs. They keep your lower leg clean and offer protection from bushes.

The right footwear is essential. *Jodhpur boots,* with a short heel, prevent your feet from slipping through the stirrup, and protect your ankles.

Did you know?
There are special clothes to wear depending on the way you ride. Western, side saddle, dressage, polo - all these have slightly different equipment.

Showing
There are some very strict rules about showing and these vary depending on the class you have entered. This outfit looks really good - neat and tidy, without any bright colours to alarm the judge! The rider has a great shirt and tie, the number around her waist is tied on with matching thread, and the boots and gloves are brown, which is correct. The showing cane completes the outfit. The pony has a lovely velvet browband - everything is spotless and looks professional!

Did you know?
Jodhpurs are named after the Indian state of Jodhpur!

Schooling

For schooling you need to be comfortable and warm. These riders, riding in the winter, have great outfits with skull caps and colourful silks over the top of them. It can be great fun to match your riding kit with your pony's tack, too.

Cross country

For jumping across country the rider needs a skull cap with a hat silk, toning jersey, a body protector, gloves and boots.

Show jumping

Our show jumper wears a lovely blue hat and blue jacket with her toning shirt and tie, and the pony's browband matches nicely.

Around the yard

There are some great fleeces and jackets to wear around the stable yard. You can get cosy quilted clothing to keep you warm when the weather turns nasty, and funky hats to keep all that bodyheat from escaping through your head!

Be seen!

Fluorescent and reflective clothing is essential if you ride on or across a road. This rider has a body tabard and arm and leg bands, and the pony has leg bands, too! Even in daylight, this clothing stands out and makes riders and ponies more visible - so always wear it!

Did you know?

Top hats can only be worn by riders in the show ring after 12 noon!

Why don't you?

See how many different coloured jodhpurs you can see at your local riding school? You may see tweed and two-tone ones, as well as the usual beige!

Meet the relatives!

We go scientific as we look at the horse's nearest and dearest!

What is a horse?

Horses have taken over 55 million years to evolve to how they look now. It was all that time ago when the very first horse, *Eohippus* (which means *dawn horse*) walked on the earth. *Eohippus* looked only a little bit like the horse we know today, but it was tiny, about the size of a fox, and had an amazing five toes on each foot. Because *Eohippus* was so small, he had to hide from predators much bigger than he was, so he learned to run faster and faster on his 20 toes. Gradually, as he ran on the middle toe, the other four on each foot got smaller and smaller.

Eohippus evolved into several distinct stages of horse, until he finally became the horse we know today, with only one hoof on each foot. Who knows whether the horse has stopped evolving - it could look very different in another 55 million years!

The missing link

Przewalski's horse is the most primitive of all the equines and resembles the horses drawn on cave walls by ancient man. Named after the Polish-born explorer who re-discovered them in 1879, this Asiatic wild horse is now extinct in the wild, but the European Endangered Species Programme is determined to keep these last wild horses alive. There are now over 2,000 in zoos and safari parks all over the world, bred from just 13 horses discovered in the 1920's. Their primitive characteristics - upright mane, mealy muzzle, dorsal and leg stripes - give them their distinct appearance. They haven't changed for millions of years!

Donkey cousins

Donkeys are similar to horses and must have shared the same ancestor. However, the donkey, or ass, evolved into animals which thrive in dry desert regions. This is why donkeys are so different to horses - they have evolved to cope with living in a different habitat and eating different food. Here are just some of the many differences.

Donkeys have...

● ...larger ears. This may be so that they can hear their friends over long desert distances, or it may help to keep them cool as the larger surface area spreads the heat.

● ...fluffy coats. Donkeys don't have grease in their coats, like horses do. They are designed to live in desert regions, so grease isn't necessary. This is why donkeys kept in Great Britain need a field shelter in their fields, to get out of the rain.

● ...boxy, upright feet. Walking on sand and stone means that donkeys need very strong hooves which don't wear down as fast as horses' do. So donkey hooves need trimming regularly - they just keep on growing instead of breaking.

● ...very different voices. Donkeys bray instead of neighing. It's a very loud sound which can travel long distances and reach their friends in the desert.

● ...different markings. Most donkeys have a pale muzzle and eye rings, as well as a cross on their back, and striped legs.

So, what else is left?

Despite their differences, horses, donkeys and zebras can mate and produce offspring. What you get depends on who the parents are!

● A *Mule* has a donkey father and a horse or pony mother.

● A *Hinny* has a horse or pony father, and a donkey mother.

● A *Zebronkey*, or a *Zeedonk* is a cross between a zebra and a donkey.

● A *Zorse* is a cross between a zebra and a horse.

Stripey friends

Zebras are the most striking of all the horse family. It is thought that their stripes offer protection against predators, as a lion would find it difficult to pick out a single animal when the herd is moving. The black and white combination may also help to keep them cool. Also, each zebra has a unique stripe pattern!

Not all zebras are the same. Just as there are breeds of horses and ponies, zebras are divided into different species. Each species has its own distinguishing set of stripes, behaviour and habitat so that they don't interbreed - so each species stays pure.

So what do you think, is the zebra a black animal with white stripes, or a white animal with black stripes?

Scientific factoid

Even though these crosses, or hybrids, can be born, their bodies cannot produce genetic material. It is because the chromosomes which live in their cells are a different shape and size to their parents, and they also have a different number. So, hybrids cannot breed - you cannot get a three-quarter mule, or three-quarter zebronkey. They only come in halves!

Why don't you?

The next time you visit a zoo or safari park, find out how many different horse relations they have there. See what you can learn about them!

Puzzle fun!

Try our horsy puzzles - see how many you can solve!

Square by square
Can you copy this horse by copying square by square?

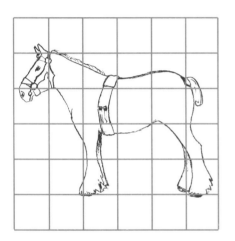

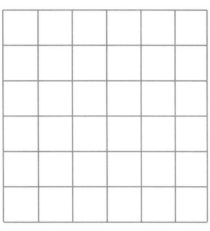

Odd one out
All of these pictures of this pony look the same - but one is different. Can you tell which one?

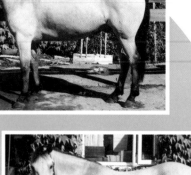

Saddle up!
Sophie wants to saddle up George and go for a ride, Can you discover which path she needs to take to get to George's stable?

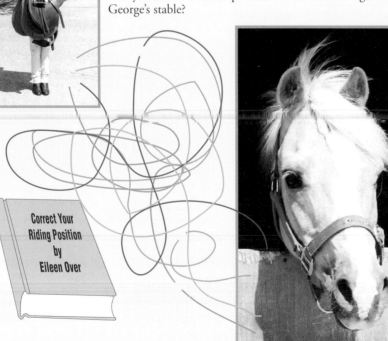

Correct Your Riding Position by Eileen Over

How many?
Study this picture, then answer the questions!
1. How many ponies can you see?
2. How many ponies with blazes can you see?
3. How many ponies are plaited?
4. How many people are wearing skull caps?
5. How many people are wearing velvet riding hats?
6. How many people in the front row are wearing short boots?
7. How many people in the front row are wearing long boots?
8. How many piebald ponies can you see?

Jump a Clear Round by Willie Klearit

Cross Country Riding by Walter Jump

Grooming kit wordsearch

Can you find all the items of grooming kit we've hidden in our wordsearch?

Words to find
SWEATSCRAPER   STABLE RUBBER   CURRY COMB
WATER BRUSH   MANE COMB   SPONGE
HOOF PICK   DANDY BRUSH

```
s w e a t s c r a p e r t
t o o v e p a i n e a c d
a r h p l o m i m n s u a
b d n n a n e h a o r r n
l e p o w g s p n t l r d
e t o e l e f m e l c y y
r n h o o f p i c k y c b
u e e l s r s t o k s o r
b l l i a e h r m s c m u
b b y t g n e e b k y b s
e u a y e d r t m c e o h
r o o d l y o a i i g r e
w a t e r b r u s h l m d
```

How many words can you make from the words
HORSES AND PONIES?

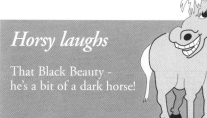

Horsy laughs

That Black Beauty -
he's a bit of a dark horse!

A magical pony walked along the road -
then turned into a field!

What do you call a donkey with three legs and one eye?
A winkey, wonkey donkey!

Missing Words

Read our story, then see if you can fill in the gaps with the words we've provided. But look out! We've added a few bogus words to our list, just to confuse you. When you have finished, you should have four spare words!

A new pony!

Kate was 1._ _ _ _ _ _ _ - she was going to pick up her new 2._ _ _ _! She had gone to see lots of ponies, but she liked the 3._ _ _ _ pony, Silver, the best. Silver had been really good when Kate had 4._ _ _ _ _ _ her, and she didn't mind traffic - Kate had to 5._ _ _ _ _ a road to get from her riding stables where Silver would live, to the woods. Kate's mum hitched up the horse trailer to the car, and they went to the 6._ _ _ _ _ _ school where Silver lived.

As they turned into the yard, they could see some girls getting Silver 7._ _ _ _ _ for her journey. Silver was wearing a lovely blue 8._ _ _ and the girls were putting travelling boots on her 9._ _ _ _. Kate knew that ponies needed protection when they travelled - they could tread on themselves, and the rug would keep Silver 10._ _ _ _ in the draughty trailer.

"Hello Kate," the owner of the stables came out to greet Kate and her mother. Kate could hardly wait to get her new pony home. She had waited ages for this day - her own pony at 11._ _ _ _ _!

Finally, Silver was ready to travel. One of the girls led her towards the ramp of the trailer - Silver walked in. It seemed as though Silver couldn't wait to see her new home! With the ramp safely secured, Kate and her mum got into their 12._ _ _ and Kate's mum drove Silver very carefully home. When they arrived, Kate led out her new pony for everyone to see. Then she put her away in her new 13._ _ _ _ _ _ . She had prepared a deep bed and an inviting 14._ _ _ _ _ _ for Silver - and then she let her alone to settle in. Silver had a lot to get used to - and Kate couldn't wait for the next day when she would ride her for the 15._ _ _ _ _ time!

Words
warm ridden cross legs rug stable bored Silver haynet excited
pony riding ready grey last car tail lorry first

Turn to page 94 to discover the answers

Gymkhana!

If you've ever wanted to enter a gymkhana, here's the lowdown on mounted games. There's more to it than collecting your rosette!

Gymkhana ponies

Good gymkhana ponies need training - they are specialists, just like top show jumpers and dressage horses. Gymkhana ponies need the ability to run fast in a straight line while their rider vaults on, to turn on a sixpence, stand waiting for the start, and the ability to get on with their team mates. Top ponies are highly prized and often stay within a Pony Club branch - just changing owners!

Gymkhana riders

To compete in mounted games riders need good hand-eye co-ordination. No good getting to the bucket first if you miss throwing the potato in it! Riders need to be fit and agile - there is a lot of vaulting on, dismounting at speed, running with your pony and leaning out of the saddle. Would you be a good mounted games rider?

What's the difference?

There is a difference between gymkhanas and mounted games. Gymkhana games are usually held at shows. Heats for each game produce a final heat, where the winners of the heats battle it out for the rosettes. At these shows you may see tiny children being led by their parents - the parents have to be fit, too! Mounted games are often held at competitions in their own right. The Mounted Games Association of Great Britain holds games throughout the country and the World Championships take place every year. Teenagers usually compete in the Championships - they are experienced, and have ponies who are really hot at the games!

This rider is just starting her gymkhana career and is being led in the dressing-up race.

The sack race requires special skills from the rider!

The bending race: this rider is still training her pony - experienced ponies gallop through the poles!

This rider has to vault on from the off side - and his team mate leads his pony.

The flag race requires the pony to turn close to the flag and the rider needs to pick it up!

Could you vault on like this - while the pony is cantering!

Sometimes the best way to carry something is to bite it - it leaves both hands free!

Did you know?

Gymkhana is a word from India. Cavalrymen stationed in India during the 19th century played games on their horses for something to do. Many of the games in gymkhanas today are based on the games these cavalrymen played to let off steam.

Why don't you?

Visit your Pony Club area or zone final of the Prince Philip Cup games. Pick a team to support and have a great day yelling your head off!

Test yourself!

Test yourself on the information we've given you between pages 46 and 67. Fill in the answers in pencil and you can rub them out and try again to improve your score!

1. Who first played gymkhana games?

_____

2. Can you match the common name with the scientific name?
a) Equus Caballus
b) Equus Zebra
c) Equus Asinus

d) Donkey
e) Horse
f) Zebra

_____

_____

_____

3. Can you name the five stages of jumping?

_____

_____

_____

_____

4. True or false
You should always put your pony's reins over his head before you put his bridle on.
☐ True   ☐ False

5. Name an association which can grant a riding school approval.

_____

6. Where do Fjord horses come from?

_____

7. Which is a pony's near side? Which is his off side?

_____

_____

8. Can you name two different Appaloosa coat patterns?

_____

_____

9. True or False
Riders can wear top hats in the show ring after 10am.
☐ True   ☐ False

10. What does Eohippus mean?

_____

_____

11. In which year did HRH Prince Philip start the Prince Philip Cup?

_____

_____

12. True or false?
Donkeys have more grease in their coats than horses.
☐ True   ☐ False

13. What is a bending race?
a) A race with poles through which the pony runs, or bends. ☐
b) A race where the rider has to bend down to pick something up. ☐
c) A race in which teams of ponies and riders bend over their pony's necks. ☐

14. Which has a donkey father - a mule or a hinny?

_____

15. How did Appaloosa horses get their name?

_____

_____

_____

16. How many legs does a horse land on after a jump?

_____

17. Put these statements about saddling up in the correct order.
a) From the near side, do up the girth
b) Check the numnah is pulled up in the arch of the saddle
c) Put the saddle on
d) Pull the buckle guard down
e) Go around the other side of the pony

_____

18. Who used to have fighting horses?

_____

19. Name two things to look for in a good riding school.

_____

_____

20. True or false
A horse cannot see a jump as he is actually jumping it.
☐ True   ☐ False

21. Can you name two ways to recognise a Fjord horse?

_____

_____

22. When did Eohippus walk the earth?
a) 25 million years ago ☐
b) 45 million years ago ☐
c) 55 million years ago ☐

23. What colour gloves should you wear in the show ring?

_____

24. Which of these are characteristics of Appaloosa horses?
a) Sparse mane ☐ right ☐ wrong
b) Big knees ☐ right ☐ wrong
c) Gentle temperament ☐ right ☐ wrong
d) Mottled muzzle ☐ right ☐ wrong
e) Striped hooves ☐ right ☐ wrong
f) Black hooves ☐ right ☐ wrong
g) Thin tails ☐ right ☐ wrong

25. Where did the word _jodhpur_ originate from?

_____

Turn to page 96 to discover the answers.
See how many times you have to do the quiz until you get every answer right!

Mares and foals

Leggy, inquisitive and as cute as a button. Horse and pony foals are just irresistible!

Springtime equals foaltime!

Springtime brings a new crop of horse and pony foals. The gestation period for a foal (the time it takes to grow in its mother) is 11 months. With the spring grass and warm weather, springtime foals can spend the summer growing up and learning how to be horses!

Instincts

Foals are usually born during the night. In the wild, mares due to foal will take themselves off to a quiet place and foal alone. They have to be careful - predators will be on the lookout for an easy meal. Because of this, horse and pony foals instinctively struggle to their feet as soon as they can - usually within an hour of being born. They have a tough time getting those long, long legs to work and balance, but they make it. They need to suckle as soon as they can, to build up their strength - and this is done instinctively, too. Needing to keep up with their mum and the rest of the herd just hours within birth, those long legs - as long as their mother's - are vital!

Boisterous

Being with a herd with other foals is great - the foals can all play with one another. If they get too boisterous, their mothers soon tell them off.

Lessons

Domestic horses, the ones we keep and ride, need to learn how to interact with humans, as well as their own kind. Stud farms, where horses are bred, copy the natural herd system by turning their mares and foals out in the field during the day. But they still handle the foals daily, so that they become used to human contact. It is very important to train foals from an early age to lead, pick their feet up, and be groomed. That way, they can easily fit in when training is taken further, and when the farrier comes to trim their feet.

Show horses even go to shows with their foals. The foals have to be at least six weeks old, and the sights and sounds at the showground are quite a lot for a youngster to take in but with mum nearby, it isn't so bad.

Maturity

Young horses take a long time to mature. A horse has to be three years old before we can ride him - and even then we have to take it slowly, as horses do not mature completely until they are six years old.

Did you know?
A mother horse is called a dam.

Did you know?
Male foals are called colt foals; female foals are called filly foals. A colt is a young male horse under three years old. A filly is a young female horse under three years old.

Why don't you?
Try to find classes for mares and foals at horse shows. Even from an early age you may see foals plaited up and being led around behind their mothers. See which ones take after their mothers!

Feeding horses and ponies

When we ride horses and ponies, they need lots of energy to do all those exciting things we want them to do. Extra food gives them this extra energy, but there are still lots of things to remember about feeding!

The rules of feeding

There are recognised rules of feeding which we need to obey!

1. Clean, fresh water must always be available.
Ponies drink between 27 - 54 litres of water every day!

2. Feed little and often.
In the wild, ponies would eat grass and leaves for most of the day. Because their stomachs are small (about the size of a football), they need to have small feeds, spread out over the day, rather than one or two big feeds. Having big feeds will cause them to get colic (tummy ache). So you need to work out how much your pony needs to eat, then divide it into small, regular feeds.

3. Feed according to work, age and temperament.
If your pony is doing a lot of work (during the school holidays, for example), he will need more energy, and therefore more food, than if he was just out in the field all day. Young, growing ponies need more food, and hot-tempered horses, like Arabians, just get more and more lively if you feed them too much.

4. Keep to the same feeding hours every day.
Ponies love routine! If you feed your pony at eight o'clock every morning, he will feel hungry at eight o'clock. Don't you get peckish when it is time for your dinner?

5. Never work your pony immediately after he has had a feed.
The stomach is near the lungs, so taking your pony for a ride immediately after he has had his feed will make him feel ill and may give him colic. Always allow him an hour's rest after a feed.

6. Feed plenty of roughage.
You know that horses and ponies live on grass in the wild, so we need to give them grass or hay in their diet, to copy this. The roughage (grass and hay) fills him up, gives him something to do, and gives him that comfortable feeling. His short feed, the one he gets in a bucket, gives him energy.

7. Introduce changes in diet gradually.
Did you know that your pony has bacteria in his digestive system, and these help him to digest his feed? If you change his diet suddenly, the bacteria get caught by surprise and can be killed off. This makes it difficult for your pony to digest his feed. So spread any changes to his diet out over several days, or even weeks to prevent this from happening.

8. Feed clean, good quality forage.
You wouldn't want to eat any food which was dusty, mouldy or past its sell-by date, would you? Well, neither would your pony!

9. Feed something succulent every day.
If your pony lives out in the field for part of the day, he will get plenty of grass. If he lives in a stable, try to give him some carrots or apples in his diet. He'll love them!

Eating pattern
Horses and ponies are not like us. They are herd animals, who have evolved to graze on grass. As there is lots of fibre in grass, and not much energy, they need to eat for 22 hours out of 24 to get enough goodness from it to live. When we keep ponies, we need to copy this way of eating as much as possible - feeding little and often.

Types of feed
There are lots of different feeds you can give your pony. There are feeds for ponies who need to lose weight, ponies who need to put weight on, ponies who lead active lives, ponies who are old and need a special diet, ponies who need extra roughage, ponies who suffer from laminitis. Most feeds come with extra minerals and vitamins added, so you can be sure your pony is getting all the nutrients he needs.

Complete feeds have everything your pony needs to keep him healthy. They may come as a coarse mix or in cube form.

Keep it fresh

Keep your feeds in a rat-and-weather-proof container. You may like to dampen your feed before giving to your pony, as it can get rid of any dust and make it more tasty.

Weigh it!

You need to feed your pony according to weight. Always weigh your feed and keep to the same amount.

Did you know?

You can tell how much your pony weighs by using a special horse and pony weightape. If you use this regularly, you will be able to tell whether your pony is gaining, or losing weight.

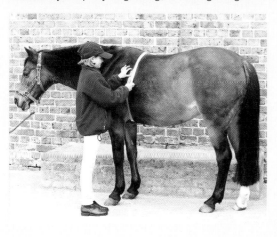

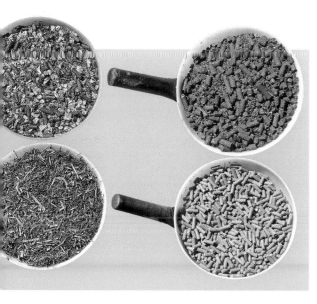

Feeding hay

Hay is important to ponies as they need the roughage and fibre it provides. Hay can be fed on the ground, or you can put it in a special haynet and hang it up in the stable. Always make sure your hay is clean and free from dust.

Did you know?

Laminits is a disease some ponies can get if they are too fat, and are on rich pasture. It affects their hooves, and makes it very painful for them to walk. You need to be very careful how you feed a pony who is prone to laminitis - look out for special feeds for laminitic ponies.

Why don't you?

Give your pony a treat every now and then. Make sure you keep your hand flat, and keep your thumb in, too, as your pony cannot see under his nose. If you don't, your pony may mistake your fingers for carrots!

At the horse show

If you ever get a chance to go to a horse show - don't miss it! It's the ideal opportunity to see all kinds of horses and ponies - and even donkeys! Join us at the horse show and discover what we can see!

Show classes

There's a bewildering number of different classes at shows - the big shows, like Hickstead and the county shows have so many, they have to hold them over several days. Look in the programme to see the different classes you can watch - and plan your day so that you don't miss your favourites.

In-hand classes

In-hand classes are for horses and ponies who are led around the show ring in front of the judge. There is a real art to showing horses and ponies in-hand - they need to be turned out properly, and every breed has a different standard. The handler needs to look good, too! Each horse has to be walked and trotted up for the judge, then asked to stand so the judge can really take a good look.

This isn't just a beauty contest - the judge will be looking for horses which are the best representation of their breed, have good conformation, and are capable of becoming good riding or driving horses. They need to have a kind temperament, too!

Did you know?

Show jumping started out as leaping competitions held by the Royal Dublin Society in Ireland in 1864.

Did you know?

There are many different show jumping classes. The Puissance comprises a spread fence and a huge wall, which is raised after every round. It is always a popular class with good prize money, and some horses specialise in Puissance classes.

Show jumping

At the big country shows, look out for the top show jumpers in action. The jumps always look huge, but the horses just sail over! See if you can find the collecting ring; here, the riders practise over the jumps, their grooms putting the poles higher or lower as instructed. Most classes have a first round, then the riders who got a clear round jump off against the clock, which is very exciting to watch. After the prize giving, the winners all gallop around the ring in a lap of honour!

Showing under saddle

These classes are many and varied. Look out for classes for hunters, hacks, cobs, coloured horses, leading rein ponies, and ridden ponies. There will also be classes for working hunters and ponies who have to jump a set of rustic jumps, then do a showing class. When showing under saddle, the horses and ponies walk, trot and canter in the ring together, then the judge calls them into a line before each one does an individual show to impress the judge. This can take a long time - most showing classes last at least an hour!

See if you can spot the different clothes the riders wear in each class - and note whether their horses wear coloured browbands, or have their manes plaited. Cobs are shown without their manes at all - they are clipped off, or *hogged*. At the big shows, there may be classes where the winners qualify to go to the *Horse of the Year Show*, at the end of the season, in October.

Did you know?

Horses need to go fast to clear spread fences, but can approach high fences slowly. See how fast they go when they approach a water jump, which is long and low, and how they slow down to do a high jump, like the Puissance wall.

Driving

Driving classes will often be included in the bigger shows. They may be

show driving classes, where the horses and carriages are judged on correctness and way of going, or they may include a carriage class and a marathon. This is where the four-in-hand go for a drive in the country, then they go through a cross country course, like a three-day-event. This is very exciting as there are lots of obstacles to negotiate. They are so narrow, the drivers need to be very experienced - the horses need to be very obedient!

Scaled down

It's not all high-powered stuff! At local shows you will see lots of smaller classes with ordinary people and horses, all having a great time. This competitor is taking part in the leading-rein gymkhana. It may be at a lower level than at the county shows, but it is just as hotly contested!

When it's all over

At the end of the day, all the horses need to be looked after and taken care of, whether they have won a rosette, or not. This top show jumper is being washed down by his groom after winning a major jumping class. All the horses and ponies who took part in the horse show will need to be fed and taken home, ready for the next horse show.

Why don't you?

Watch showing classes at shows and pretend to be the judge. See if the real judge agrees with your final choice!

Why don't you?

Remember to take your autograph book with you to the bigger shows - then you can see how many famous show jumping names you can collect.

The Thoroughbred

Which is the world's fastest horse? Which breed descended from just three founder stallions? Which breed competes in The Sport of Kings? The Thoroughbred! We take a closer look at the world's equine running machine.

History

English kings and queens have always loved racing and during the 17th and 18th century the monarchy and their nobles became even more addicted to *The Sport of Kings*. These 'running horses', as they were known, were a mixture of different breeds, including Scottish-bred Galloway ponies. Three founder stallions were discovered, and brought to England. These sires founded the entire Thoroughbred breed we know today.

Three founder stallions

The Byerley Turk was captured by Captain Byerley in 1683 at the siege of Vienna. This Arab horse carried the Captain in lots of further battles, before going to England in 1691 and standing at stud.

The Godolphin Barb came from Tunis but was discovered pulling a water cart through the streets of Paris in 1729 by Edward Coke, who took the horse to England. When Edward Coke died, he left the horse to Roger Williams, who bought and sold racehorses. He sold the horse, whose name was Sham, to Lord Godolphin's stud. The Godolphin Barb died on Christmas Day 1753, aged 29.

Thomas Darley, the British Consul in Aleppo, Syria, exchanged a gun for a horse which became known as the Darley Arabian, giving him to his brother, Richard. This beautiful stallion reached England in 1704 and stood at stud at the Darley estate in Yorkshire. This stallion lived to be 30 years old. Amazingly, 95% of all English Thoroughbreds are descended from him! These three remarkable stallions founded the Thoroughbred dynasty - all modern Thoroughbreds can trace their ancestry back through the lines founded by these three stallions!

Racehorses

Most pure-bred Thoroughbreds are racehorses. Flat racers race early on in their lives, and Thoroughbreds are born early in the year as they all take their birthday from January 1st. Racehorses who compete in steeplechases or hurdle races are usually bigger than flat racers, and need to be stronger and tougher.

How to spot a Thoroughbred

Originated in: Great Britain and Ireland.
Colours: Solid colours only. Bay and chestnut are most common - black, brown and grey are also seen.
Height: Between 15hh - 16.2hh.
How to spot a Thoroughbred: Look for a lean running machine! Long in the body and light in build, the Thoroughbred has a noble and elegant presence. The legs are long and the quarters, where the engine and muscle power lie, are strong and powerful. The head is refined and graceful.
Is a Thoroughbred for you? Highly bred, Thoroughbreds are nervous and temperamental creatures with well-developed senses. They need calm and experienced riders who can cope with their character. With a love of going fast, you need plenty of riding room with a Thoroughbred!

Thoroughbred Factoid
The name Thoroughbred is often shortened to TB.

Thoroughbred Factoid
During a race, a Thoroughbred's heart-rate can increase from 25 to 250 beats per minute. Amazing!

Schooling a pony

Even ponies have to go to school! Just as we have lessons to learn the things we need to know, ponies need lessons in the school or manège to learn to do what their riders want them to do. We joined Sophie and Violet on their schooling session.

Streeeetch!

Sophie begins her schooling session by walking Violet around to stretch her legs and loosen her up. Violet has been in her stable all night, so she may be a bit stiff - just as we are when we first get out of bed.

Trotting

Once Violet is warmed up, Sophie asks her to trot. She wants Violet to trot briskly, without hurrying, and she needs to trot exactly when Sophie asks her to. Changing pace is called making a *transition*, and Sophie wants Violet to make her transitions as soon as she asks for them. An upward transition is when Violet goes from a slower pace to a faster pace (from walk to trot, for example). A downward transition is when she goes from a faster pace to a slower pace.

Did you know?

If a pony misbehaves, he's probably trying to tell you something! It could be that his tack is hurting him - always check this out if your pony is naughty. Check his teeth and back, too - if his teeth are too long, they will bang on the bit. If his back is sore, the saddle and your weight will hurt him. Or - it could be that he is tired. Try to think of every reason why your pony could be naughty - they usually like to please us!

Change of rein

It is important for ponies to work equally on both reins. This means that they should do the same amount of work on the left rein (going around to the left), as they do on the right rein (going around to the right). If they do more work on one rein, they can become one-sided.

Did you know?
Ponies get bored and tired - just like us! This is why it is important to keep schooling sessions short.

Did you know?
Dressage is the ultimate schooling! The word comes from the French verb *dresser* and means to train or adjust.

Time to canter

Canter work is always fun - but Sophie has to make sure Violet doesn't get too tired. Again, the transition from trot to canter is important, and Sophie concentrates on keeping the canter steady and rhythmic. No galloping about!

Why don't you?

If you are schooling your own pony, remember to keep smiling. This ensures you do not tense up - which is very easy to do when you are concentrating so hard. This can make your pony tense, too!

Break time

Sophie asks Violet for some turns and circles, as she trots. She also makes sure her pony doesn't get tired or bored - here she has asked her to walk and have a breather before going on to the next part of her schooling programme.

Well done!
With her schooling session over, Sophie makes sure Violet knows how pleased she is with her. Violet has worked really well, so Sophie is going to put her away and give her some feed as a reward.

Horse markings

Horses and ponies often have facial or leg markings. If you want to be a pony expert, you'll need to know them all!

Brands

You may see these brands on various breeds of horses and ponies.

Freezemarking

This is an identification mark in case the horse is lost or stolen. The brand is applied cold, so it kills the hairs without hurting the horse.

Exmoor ponies can be identified by this special Exmoor brand.

Pure bred Haflinger ponies all have this brand.

Hanovarian horses are branded like this.

Breed brands show that the horse or pony is purely bred and gives it identification throughout its life.

This is a Trakehner brand.

Face markings

White chin
Just a white patch on the chin.

White muzzle
This pony has a white muzzle and a white chin. Look out for pink flesh markings on the white bits, too!

Snip
This is a small white marking between the nostrils.

Whorls

Look for tiny areas where the hair goes in a whorl - a circle of hair. These can be found on the head, the neck, the chest and the flanks, and are like human fingerprints - a form of identification.

Stocking
This white marking extends over the knee.

White leg
This can be described according to where the white extends to - half white cannon, for example.

White pastern
A white marking over the fetlock.

Leg markings

  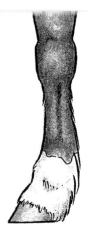

Star and snip
A white star
between the eyes,
as well as a snip.

Star
A patch of white hair
between the eyes.

Stripe
This narrow
white stripe runs
from the forehead
to the muzzle.

Blaze
A wide, white
stripe, extending
over one or both
nostrils.

White face
This broad white marking extends
over the eye. This pony has a wall eye
- where the brown pigmentation of
the eye is blue. It is quite common
on white faced, and cream ponies,
and the sight is unaffected.

Why don't you?
Next time you are at a horse show, see how many different face and leg
markings you can identify. If you see some breed classes, see if you can
spot the brands we have shown here!

Dorsal stripe
Again, found on duns and
some light bay horses and
ponies. Also known as an
eel stripe.

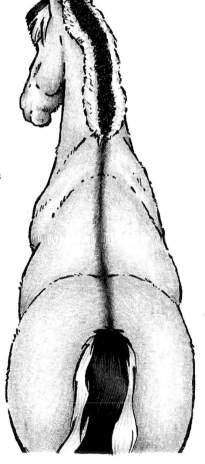

Sock
A white marking
to the fetlock.

White coronet
A thin white
marking around
the coronet.

White heel
Just a smudge
of white.

Ermine marks
Black marks
on a white leg.

Zebra stripes
These are often found on
dun ponies. The dark stripes
are often faint but can be
clearly seen.

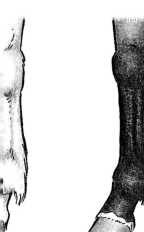

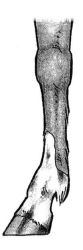

A day at the vet's

Danielle has taken her horse, Roscoe, to have his annual health check at the veterinary surgery. This is to make sure Roscoe is healthy and well, and to update his vaccinations.

Quick march

Vet Stuart Duncan watches Roscoe trot up in front of him. The horse is fully sound - so no problems there!

Eye, eye

An examination of Roscoe's eyes ensures his eyes are healthy. The special instrument can look at the inner eye. Roscoe's eyes are fine!

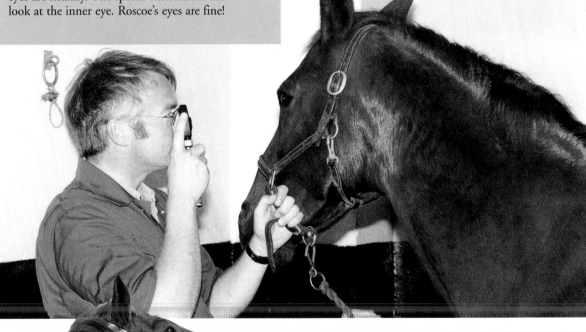

Horse dentistry

Now to Roscoe's teeth. Sharp edges can cause ulcers and sores in the mouth. Stuart sees that Roscoe's teeth do have some sharp edges, so......

...he let's Danielle have a feel! The gag keeps Roscoe's mouth open so that he can't bite anyone. Stuart can then file the teeth down using a special rasp. Roscoe will be much more comfortable, and he will be able to eat easier - which he will enjoy!

Time to be brave!

It is time for Roscoe's tetanus and equine influenza vaccination. Tetanus is a bacteria which lives in the soil and can make the horse really ill if it gets in a cut or wound. Few horses who get tetanus recover so it is vital for Roscoe to get this vaccination. Equine flu is like human flu - and as Roscoe goes to lots of horse shows, and meets other horses and ponies, this is a good vaccination for him to have. It will prevent him for catching the virus and being ill for several weeks. Once Roscoe has his jab, his vaccination certificates are filled in by Stuart. You can see Roscoe has had lots of vaccinations - one every year.

To the lab

Stuart also took a sample of Roscoe's blood. This goes to the laboratory for analysis by the lab technician. The test will let Stuart know whether Roscoe is suffering from anaemia, and it can detect other problems which are not obvious.

Roscoe is certainly getting a thorough health check!

Listening in

Stuart listens to Roscoe's heart rate with a stethoscope. His breathing is fine - any abnormalities may indicate that Roscoe is suffering from a condition which is similar to asthma in humans.

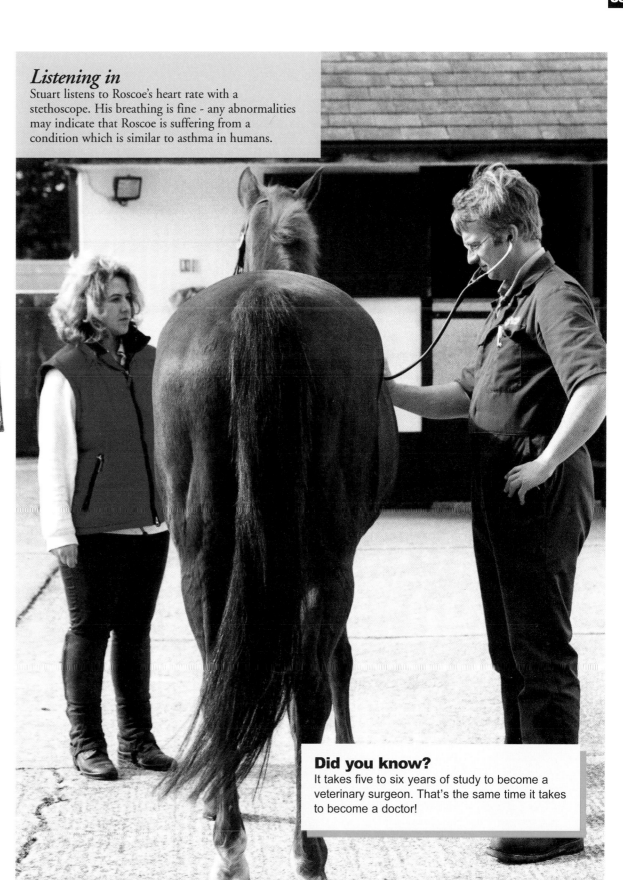

Did you know?

It takes five to six years of study to become a veterinary surgeon. That's the same time it takes to become a doctor!

Puzzle fun!

Here are some more great horsy puzzles to solve!

Square by square
Can you draw this pony by copying square by square?

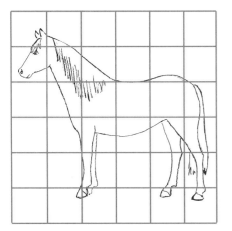

Odd one out
Which of these is the odd one out - and why?

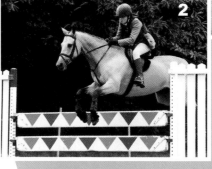

Which path
Lucy and Sue are waiting for Miggy to catch them up. Can you tell which path Miggy needs to take to reach her friends?

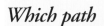

Can't Stop Grooming by Ivor Brush

How many?
Study this picture, then answer the questions
1. How many grey ponies are there?
2. How many palomino ponies are there?
3. How many ponies have blazes?
4. How many of the riders are wearing pink?
5. How many riders have riding crops?
6. How many ponies are chestnut?
7. How many of the riders are wearing waistcoats?
8. How many riders are wearing the colour purple?

Breaking a Horse to Harness by G G Driver

Horse names wordsearch

Can you find all the horses' names we've hidden in our wordsearch?

Words to find

PRINCE   GEORGE   CHEYENNE
SMARTY   JIGSAW   CAPTAIN
TRIGGER   SIMON   SILVER
SMOKEY   STARLIGHT   MAGPIE

```
c a p t a i n o u k e d t
h o o v e i a s m a r t y
e m a g p i c i a n s t m
y d n n a j i g s a w i s
e e p o w n s p v t l m t
n s t a r l i g h t c s o
n n p t c t i u i e y t g
e e e l s r p s s k s r e
t r i g g e r m m s c e o
g b y t g n i l o k y b r
i u s i m o n k k c e o g
n o o d l y c e e i g r e
l g s i l v e r y n l m d
```

How many words can you make from the words
SADDLE SOAP

Horsy laughs

What does it mean if you find a horse shoe?
Some poor horse is walking around in his socks!

When do vampires like horse racing?
When it's neck and neck!

What do you call a donkey with three legs, one eye and BO?
A winkey, wonkey, honkey, donkey!

Missing words

Read our story, then see if you can fill in the gaps with the words we've provided. But beware! We've added a few bogus words to confuse you. When you've finished, you should have four spare words!

First dressage test!

Sarah had entered her pony, Toffee, for a
1. _ _ _ _ _ _ _ _ test at their riding school. They had never competed in dressage before, but Sarah and
2. _ _ _ _ _ _ had been having lots of **3.** _ _ _ _ _ _ _ and Sarah was looking forward to the
4. _ _ _ _ _ _ _ _ _ _ _ . The first thing Sarah had to do was learn the test. She got a copy of it from her
5. _ _ _ _ _ _ _ _ _ _ and spent a few evenings looking at it, and memorising it. After a week, however, she was still having trouble **6.** _ _ _ _ _ _ _ _ _ _ _ it. Her instructor had a good **7.** _ _ _ _ .

"Why don't you mark out a dressage arena on a
8. _ _ _ _ _ of paper, then go through it with a model pony. You can do this on a table or in the garden and it really helps you to **9.** _ _ _ _ _ the test!" Sarah thought

she would try it, so she got out one of her
10. _ _ _ _ _ ponies, and went into the garden. It really did work - after just a few times, she was getting the hang of the test. Now she was ready to practise on Toffee!

Toffee was a very willing pony - Sarah loved him to bits - and they went through the transitions and
11. _ _ _ _ _ _ _ _ _ they would need to do in the dressage test. Their instructor was pleased with them.

"You both look great. Now just go out and enjoy yourselves!"

On the day of the dressage competition, Sarah was very **12.** _ _ _ _ _ _ _ . She plaited Toffee's **13.** _ _ _ _ , got herself ready, and **14.** _ _ _ _ _ _ _ _ _ her number.

"We'll do our best ,Toffee," Sarah whispered, as they entered the arena. Sarah remembered her test and Toffee went really well. They came out of the arena feeling great.

"We did it, Toffee!" Sarah cried, "**15.** _ _ _ _ boy!"

Words

dressage instructor competition piece model idea bad learn Toffee movements jumped good mane number remembering forgetting nervous collected lessons

Turn to page 94 to discover the answers

Horse talk

Do you know what horses and ponies are thinking? How can you tell?
Follow our easy-to-follow guide to be fluent in horse talk in no time!

Body talk

To tell what your pony is saying, you need to remember that horses communicate through body talk. Humans do, too - only we depend so much on talking, we sometimes don't realise we are using our body to communicate as well. So, when you want to know what your pony is thinking, or saying to other ponies, you need to take into account his body. Look at his head, especially; this tells you a lot about how your pony is feeling.

Riding talk

Watch ponies when they are being ridden - their facial expressions give away what they are thinking. Can you tell what this ridden pony is thinking about?

One: Clues - ears forward, eyes looking bright, head up.

"I'm concentrating on something over there - so don't expect me to be thinking about you and what you are telling me from the saddle."

If your pony has his ears forward when you are riding him, he isn't listening to you!

Two: Clues - ears resting, eyes sleepy, head lowered.

"I'm concentrating on you. So, if you are telling me to do something, I will do my best."

When the ears are sideways like this, your pony is thinking about what his rider is asking him to do. That's why ears in this position are somethimes called *listening ears*!

Three: Clues - ears back, eyes showing white, nose poked forward.

"I'm angry! That horse next to me is too close and I'm thinking of biting or kicking him!"

There is a difference between the ears in this picture, and in picture two. This expression is one of anger - your pony is cross, so look out!

From the ground

You can see the expressions on your pony's face much clearer when you are on the ground and leading him. Can you tell what this pony is saying?

One: Clues - one ear back, eyes not focused to the front.

"There is something going on behind me - but there is also a sound in front of me, too. I'll keep an ear on both!"

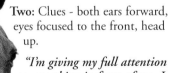

Two: Clues - both ears forward, eyes focused to the front, head up.

"I'm giving my full attention to something in front of me. I hope it's a bucket of feed!"

Three: Clues - both ears forward, whites of the eyes showing.

"I don't like the look of what's going on over there - I think I might try to make a run for it soon!"

What are they saying?

So, you can now see how many different expressions horses and ponies have. See if you can tell what the ones pictured here are saying. We've written the answers upside down so you can check them after you have worked it out!

"Where's my dinner!"

"I'm tired - I think I'll have a quick doze."

"Look out, I'm going to kick you!"

"I think my door's too big!"

Did you know?

This expression is often seen when a horse has smelt something it likes. It is known as the *Flehmen* expression.

Why don't you?

Take a look at the expressions on the faces of horses and ponies you meet - and see if you can tell what they are saying!

The Lipizzaner

The white horses of the Spanish Riding School of Vienna, the Lipizzaner has a romantic and colourful history.

History

The stud at Lipizza, which was then part of the Austrian Empire, was founded as long ago as 1580. The stud supplied horses to the Royal court stables in Vienna. Eight years before, the Spanish Riding School in Vienna had been established. It was called the Spanish Riding School because it used Spanish horses. As the original type of Spanish horses became difficult to find, the horses were bred with Neapolitan horses from Germany and Denmark. Arab blood was introduced later on and this was the foundation of the famous Lipizzaner breed. Six foundation stallions all have descendants at the present Spanish Riding School of Vienna!

Colour influence

The stud at Lipizza bred mainly white horses - because it was considered the most dignified colour for the Imperial court. Until the 18th century, however, other colours were common. Colours such as black, bay, dun, cream, and even spotted and broken-coloured horses were seen. Today, Lipizzaners are almost always grey - although referred to as white - with some bays. A bay stallion is kept to perform at the Riding School, together with all the greys, although bays are not used for breeding.

Built for ballet

The conformation of the Lipizzaner horse makes it perfect for high school work, known as *Haute École*, a mixture of equestrian gymnastics and ballet. With its intelligence and willing temperament, the Lipizzaner excels at the difficult and beautiful movements which earned it the name of the dancing white horses. The riders all dress in traditional costume, the horses wear old fashioned saddlery, and the sight of the horses and riders in perfect harmony is one difficult to forget.

A long training time

Training each stallion takes four years - and the specialised leaps, known as the *airs above the ground* - take longer still. Only the most talented horses are selected to train for these. The movements are based on how horses were trained to protect and help their rider during warfare. They are graceful and very difficult to do which is why the training takes so long. The horses need to develop the powerful muscles needed to help them carry out the leaps, and they cannot be hurried.

How to spot a Lipizzaner

Originated in: Vienna, Austria.
Colours: Grey - occasionally bay.
Height: About 15hh.
How to spot a Lipizzaner: The Lipizzaner is a stocky, powerful horse. Some may have an Arab looking head - others may look more Spanish. They have huge, dark eyes. The limbs are short and muscular, ideal for the work they do.
Is a Lipizzaner for you? These romantic-looking horses are intelligent and kind. They are easy to teach - they love their work. If you want a horse with history, who is willing to work for you and is kind and gentle, the Lipizzaner is for you!

Lipizzaner Factoid

The present riding school, built in 1729, is a beautiful arena where regular performances are given to the public. The Spanish Riding School also tours to perform in other parts of the world. If you ever get a chance to see the dancing white horses - don't miss it!

Lipizzaner Footoid

Since 1920, Lipizanners have been bred at Piber, in Austria.

Lipizzaner Factoid

Lipizzaner foals are all born black or brown - they gradually turn white with age!

Horsy makes for you to try!

Our horsy makes are not too difficult - but look great!

Make a horseshoe picture frame

Why not turn an old horseshoe that your pony doesn't want into a picture frame?

You will need
A horseshoe
Ribbon
Picture of your pony
Silver spray paint

1 Cut the picture into the same shape as the horseshoe.

2 Being very careful, spray the horseshoe silver. Remember to put it on newspaper first, so that you don't spray anything else!

3 Now thread the ribbon through the top holes in the horseshoe. The picture frame is ready to hang up!

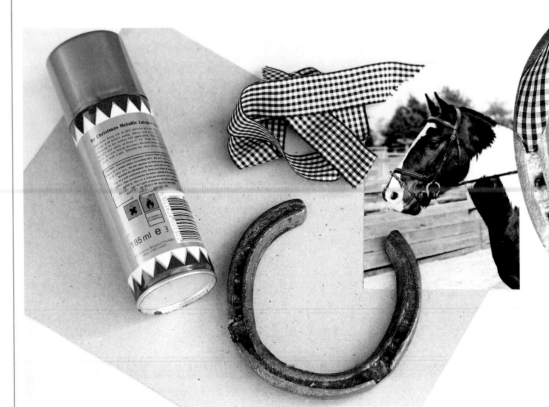

Why don't you?
Make a horseshoe picture frame for a friend with a picture of their pony in it?

Make a pony backpack

This pony will follow you everywhere - and he'll even tell you where you've been!

You will need
A backpack
Some fun-fur fabric. We found some great skewbald fabric!
Cardboard
Narrow ribbon
Paper
Felt
Wool
Glue

3 Make a mane. Stick some ribbon to a piece of cardboard. Then, put more glue on the ribbon. Wind wool around the card. When the glue is dry, and the wool is stuck to the ribbon, cut the top of the wool above the ribbon. Then peel the cardboard away. You will be left with a ribbon and a wool mane stuck to it. Stick this to your horse's neck.

4 Make a tail - wind wool around a bigger piece of cardboard, but don't use any glue. Tie another piece of wool around the tail, then cut just above it. Make a small forelock the same way.

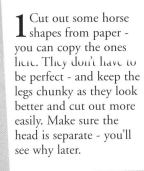

1 Cut out some horse shapes from paper - you can copy the ones here. They don't have to be perfect - and keep the legs chunky as they look better and cut out more easily. Make sure the head is separate - you'll see why later.

2 Pin the paper patterns to the fur fabric, and carefully cut round. Then cut two more legs, using the same pattern.

5 Now carefully glue the horse pieces to the backpack. Put the head on first, then the front legs - and tuck the mane down behind the body piece.

6 Now all you need to do is add the tail with glue and stick on some hooves, eyes and nostrils made from black felt. You've got a friend who will follow you everywhere!

Why don't you?
Make a backpack for a friend - and make a different colour pony!

Test yourself!

Test yourself on the features between pages 70 and 91. If you use a pencil to answer the questions, you can rub them out and try the quiz again and again!

1. What is the gestation period of a mare?

_____

2. Name two different types of showing classes.

_____

_____

3. True or false?
A horse can drink up to 54 litres of water every day.
☐ True ☐ False

4. How should you start a schooling session on your pony?
a) Walk around to loosen and supple your pony. ☐
b) Trot a few circuits to wake your pony up. ☐
c) Stand in the middle of the school and do some exercises. ☐

5. How many famous stallions founded the Thoroughbred breed?

_____

6. If your pony misbehaves during a schooling session, what should you check?

_____

_____

7. Why is the Spanish Riding School so called, even though it is in Austria?

_____

_____

_____

8. Name a vaccination your pony should have.

_____

9. Identify the following facial markings.

_____

_____

_____

10. What is a male foal called?

_____

11. What is *Haute École*?

_____

_____

12. How old does a foal have to be before it can go to a horse show?

_____

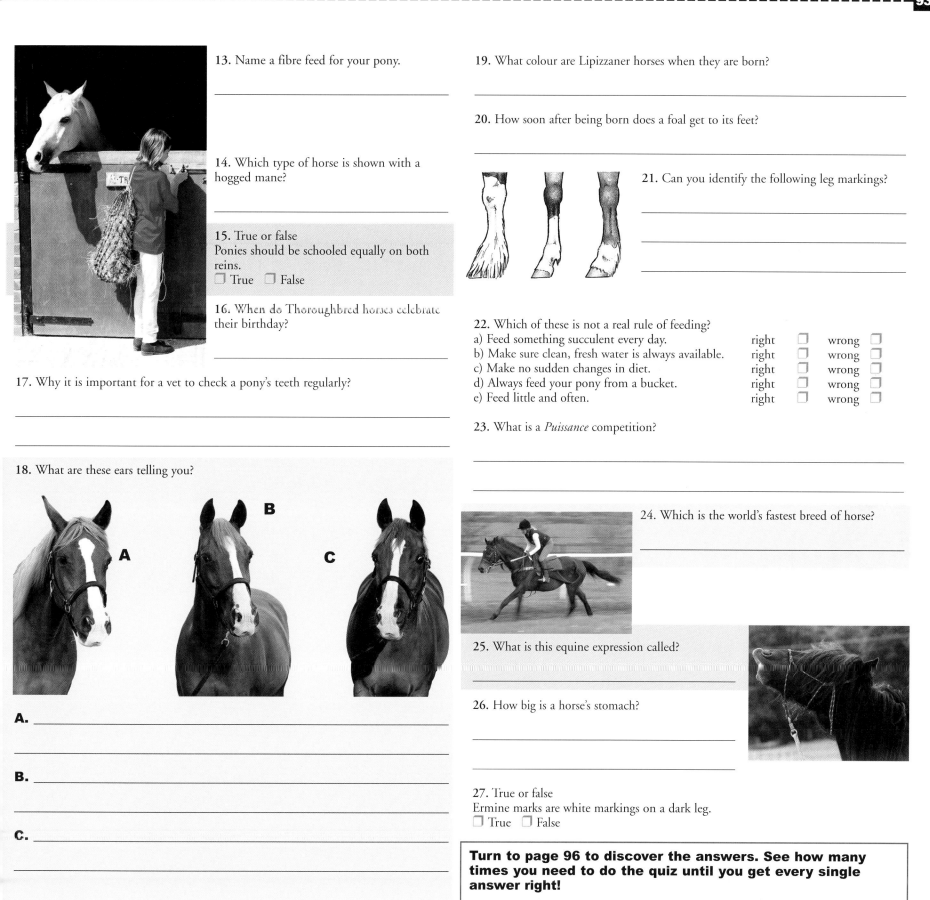

13. Name a fibre feed for your pony.

_____

14. Which type of horse is shown with a hogged mane?

_____

15. True or false
Ponies should be schooled equally on both reins.
☐ True   ☐ False

16. When do Thoroughbred horses celebrate their birthday?

_____

17. Why it is important for a vet to check a pony's teeth regularly?

_____
_____

18. What are these ears telling you?

A. _____
_____

B. _____
_____

C. _____
_____

19. What colour are Lipizzaner horses when they are born?

_____

20. How soon after being born does a foal get to its feet?

_____

21. Can you identify the following leg markings?

_____
_____
_____

22. Which of these is not a real rule of feeding?
a) Feed something succulent every day.   right ☐   wrong ☐
b) Make sure clean, fresh water is always available.   right ☐   wrong ☐
c) Make no sudden changes in diet.   right ☐   wrong ☐
d) Always feed your pony from a bucket.   right ☐   wrong ☐
e) Feed little and often.   right ☐   wrong ☐

23. What is a _Puissance_ competition?

_____
_____

24. Which is the world's fastest breed of horse?

_____

25. What is this equine expression called?

_____

26. How big is a horse's stomach?

_____
_____

27. True or false
Ermine marks are white markings on a dark leg.
☐ True   ☐ False

Turn to page 96 to discover the answers. See how many times you need to do the quiz until you get every single answer right!

Here are the answers!

How did you do with our great puzzles? Find out here and now!

....

Answers to the puzzles on pages 20 - 21.

Did you get them all right?

Let me out!
Blaze needs to take the blue path to reach his companions in the field.

Odd one out
Number six is the odd one out as it is a man-made freeze brand. All the other markings are natural.

How many?
1. 26 legs - 16 pony and 10 human.
2. One pony is wearing a flash noseband.
3. There are two grey ponies.
4. There is one chestnut pony.
5. One pony has white socks.
6. Three riders are carrying sticks.
7. Two ponies are wearing martingales.

Colour Wordsearch

```
j n j o p l j o u k e d t
n c h e s t n u t e a h i
e l h p l e b i a n s t m
p r p i e b a l d o r i s
u o p o w n y p v t l m t
o n o b l h f m u l c s o
c g b l u e r o a n g t c
l r e a s r t r k r r r
e e l c a e h r a s e e e
g y s k e w b a l d y b a
i u a y e d r o m c e o m
n o o d l y o u i i g r e
l p a l o m i n o n l m d
```

Missing words
Here are the words that were missing from the story
1. jumping
2. Welsh
3. plaiting
4. breakfast
5. trailer
6. number
7. hat
8. jump
9. reins
10. heart
11. swish
12. squeal
13. clear
14. patted

The bogus words were lunch, whip, bridle and Scottish.

Answers to the puzzles on pages 50 - 51.

Where's my breakfast?
Dinky's owner needs to take the red path to get to Dinky and feed him his breakfast.

Odd one out
Number three is the odd one out. The others all have nosebands on their bridles.

How many?
1. There are four ponies in the picture. As you can hardly see one of them, three will be accepted as a correct answer, too!
2. Four people are riding.
3. Three people appear to be walking.
4. Two people are wearing red.
5. Two people are wearing backpacks.
6. Four people are wearing riding hats.
7. One person is wearing stripes.
8. One person is wearing shorts
9. There is one grey pony.

Breed Wordsearch

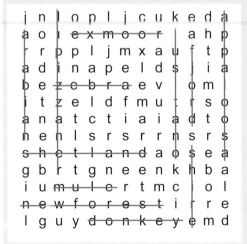

```
j n l o p l j o u k e d a
a o l e x m o o r l a h p
r r p l j m x a u f t p
a d i n a p e l d s j i a
b e z e b r a e v l o m
l t z e l d f m u t r s o
a n a t c t i a i a d t o
h e h l s r s r r m s r s
s h e t l a n d a o s e a
g b r t g n e e n k h b a
i u m u l e r t m c l o l
n e w f o r e s t i r r e
l g u y d o n k e y e m d
```

Missing words

The words missing in the story are as follows.
1. ride
2. palomino
3. white
4. grooming
5. hat
6. still
7. rock
8. saddle
9. hacking
10. farm
11. shining
12. singing
13. patted
14. snorted
15. forward
16. gallop
17. eyes
18. walk
19. hot

The bogus words were gloves, cold, wind and birds.

Answers to the puzzles on pages 64 - 65.

Saddle Up!
Sophie needs to take the green path to reach George's stable.

Odd one out
Pony number three is the odd one out.

How many?
1. You can see four ponies in the picture.
2. There are two ponies with blazes.
3. Three ponies are plaited.
4. There are five people wearing skull caps (two have covers - one velvet, one silk)
5. There are four people wearing velvet riding hats.
6. There are seven people in the front row wearing short boots.
7. There is one person in the front row wearing long boots.
8. There is one piebald pony.

Grooming kit wordsearch

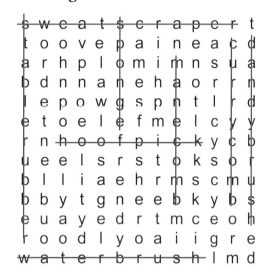

Missing words

The missing words were
1. excited
2. pony
3. grey
4. ridden
5. cross
6. riding
7. ready
8. rug
9. legs
10. warm
11. last
12. car
13. stable
14. haynet
15. first.

The bogus words were bored, tail, lorry and Silver.

Answers to the puzzles on pages 84 - 85.

Which path?
Miggy needs to take the pink path to reach her friends.

Odd one out
Picture three is the odd one out. The combination are tackling a cross country fence, the others are all competing in showjumping.

How many?
1. There are two grey ponies.
2. There are two palomino ponies.
3. Two ponies have blazes.
4. One rider is wearing pink.
5. One rider has a riding crop.
6. One pony is chestnut.
7. One rider is wearing a waistcoat.
8. One rider is wearing purple.

Horses names wordsearch

Missing words
The missing words were
1. dressage
2. Toffee
3. lessons
4. competition.
5. instructor
6. remembering
7. idea
8. piece
9. learn
10. model
11. movements
12. nervous
13. mane
14. collected
15. good

The bogus words were bad, forgetting, jumped and number.

Answers!

Here are the answers to our quiz pages!

Pages 26 & 27

1. The points are
a. Wither
b. Loins
c. Point of hock
d. Chestnut
e. Shoulder
f. Forelock.

2. A pony carries two-thirds of his bodyweight on his front legs.

3. The hoofpick should be used in the direction of heel to toe - so the answer is false.

4. The Shetland pony can be all these colours.

5. Hang a horseshoe with the ends pointing upwards to avoid the luck falling out.

6. The following statements about your riding position are all correct.
a) Sit tall d) Look up and ahead e) Allow your legs to hang close to your pony's sides g) Have equal weight on both seat bones. The other letters, b, c f and h were wrong.

7. The Arabian has all these characteristics.

8. Racehorse trainers like Thoroughbreds who have a long-striding walk because they think they will also be able to gallop!

9. The item is a metal *curry comb* and it should be used to clean a body brush.

10. Bits can be made from stainless steel, copper, rubber and vulcanite.

11. Shetland ponies have large nostrils to warm up cold air before it reaches their lungs.

12. The answer is false. Ponies need their hooves trimmed every six - eight weeks.

13. The walk is a stride of four beats.

14. The Bedouin tribes keep their Arabian horses in their own tents.

15. A Loriner makes bits.

16. Shetland ponies may eat seaweed.

17. Horses and ponies need to wear shoes because, when we ride them, their feet wear down faster than they can grow again.

18. False. A long-striding walk on a long rein is not a collected walk. A collected walk is where the horse takes short, high steps, with plenty of energy.

19. The grooming brushes should be matched as follows.
a) Dandy brush - brushes away mud and sweat.
b) Body brush, brushing manes and tails.
c) Sponge - cleaning eyes and noses.
d) Water brush - laying the mane.

20. Clenches are horseshoe nails.

21. Choose three bits from this list.
Snaffle, weymouth, curb, bridoon and pelham.

22. True - the Arabian has fewer ribs and tail bones than other horses.

23. It takes a farrier over four years to train and become qualified.

24. A body brush should not be used on a pony living out as it removes the natural grease from its coat.

25. A double bride has two separate bits.

Page 44 & 45

1. There are three beats to the stride in canter.

2. The world's tallest and heaviest horse is the Shire.

3. The correct aids to canter are:
a) Sit to the trot d) use the inside leg at the girth e) use the outside leg behind the girth. The others were all wrong.

4. The horses were skewbald, piebald, dun and palomino.

5. The best fencing you can have around a pony's field is post and rail.

6. The Ancient Romans prized the horses of Iberia.

7. A western girth is called a cinch.

8. Side saddle riders wear their hair in a bun.

9. Choose three chores you would need to do for your pony every day from these:
Feed and water, groom him, turn out in field, check water in field, bring pony in at night, muck out, ride him, clean tack.

10. When rising to the trot the rider sits on the outside diagonal.

11. There were only 2000 Shires in the 1960's.

12. A dressage saddle has a straight saddle flap and a girth fastening below the flaps.

13. True. Piaffe is a highly collected trot.

14. The average weight of a Shire horse is a tonne.

15. The Lusitano is the native horse of Portugal.

16. True. You should always leave the top half of a stable door open because ponies love fresh air.

17. When cantering the rider sits up tall and still in the saddle, allowing the lower body to follow the movement of the horse.

18. Choose three grey colourings from iron grey, dappled grey, fleabitten grey and rose grey.

19. False. Spanish *mares* are hogged and docked.

20. Points are a) colouring of the mane, tail, legs and ears.

21. The points of the saddle shown were:
a. Cantle
b. Stirrup leather
c. Girth strap
d. Stirrup
e. Pommel.

22. The Andalucian is now known as The Spanish Horse.

23. A side saddle has two pommels.

24. Choose two types of bedding from woodshavings, straw and shredded paper.

Pages 68 & 69

1. Cavalrymen in India first played gymkhana games.

2. The following matched:
a with e, b with f and c with d.

3. The five stages of jumping are: approach, take off, moment of suspension, landing and getaway.

4. True. You should always put your pony's reins over his head before you put his bridle on.

5. Two associations can grant approval to riding schools. The British Horse Society and the Association of British Riding Schools

6. Fjord horses come from Norway.

7. The pony's near side is his left side. The off side is his right side.

8. Choose two Appaloosa coat pattern from the following: snowflake, leopard, blanket, marbleized and frost.

9. False. Riders can only wear top hats in the show ring after 12 noon.

10. Eohippus means *Dawn Horse*.

11. HRH Prince Philip initiated the Prince Philip Cup in 1957.

12. False. Donkeys have far less grease in their coats than horses.

13. A bending race is a) A race with poles through which the pony runs, or bends.

14. A mule has a donkey father.

15. Appaloosa horses got their name from the Palouse river.

16. A horse lands on only one leg after he jumps.

17. The statements about saddling should have been put in the following order:
c, e, a, d and b.

18. The Vikings used to have fighting horses.

19. Choose from the following:
Approval, organised lessons, organised yard, well cared-for ponies, safe tack, friendly staff, organised office, tidy tools, tidy muck heap, well fenced paddocks and clean water troughs, clean yards, and everyone enjoying their lessons.

20. True. A horse cannot see a jump when he is actually jumping it.

21. Choose from the following characteristics of Fjord horses.
Upright mane, dorsal stripe, dun colouring, zebra leg markings.

22. Eohippus walked on the earth 55 million years ago.

23. You should wear brown gloves in the show ring.

24. Choosing characteristics of Appaloosa horses, you should have included the following.
a, d, e and g. b and f were wrong.

25. The word *Jodhpur* is from India.

Pages 92 & 93

1. The gestation period of a mare is 11 months.

2. There are in-hand or under saddle showing classes.

3. True. A horse can drink up to 54 litres of water every day.

4. You should start your schooling session by (a) walking around to loosen and supple your pony.

5. Three famous stallions founded the Thoroughbred breed.

6. If your pony misbehaves check his tack, his teeth and his back.

7. The Spanish Riding School of Vienna is so called because they used to use Spanish horses.

8. Your pony should have flu and tetanus vaccinations.

9. The facial markings are a stripe, a blaze and a white face.

10. A male foal is called a colt foal.

11. *Haute École* means high school.

12. A foal must be six weeks old before it can go to a horse show.

13. Hay is a fibre feed for your pony.

14. A cob is shown with a hogged mane.

15. True. Ponies should be schooled equally on both reins.

16. Thoroughbred horses celebrate their birthday on January 1.

17. You should check a pony's teeth regularly for sharp edges which can cause sores and ulcers.

18. The ears are saying...
a "...there is something going on behind me."
b "...I have my full attention on something in front of me."
c "...I don't like what's going on over there!"

19. Lipizzaner horses are born black or brown.

20. A foal gets to its feet within an hour of being born.

21. The leg markings are: a stocking, a white leg and a white pastern.

22. a, b, c, and e are all rules of feeding. d is not a rule.

23. A Puissance competition comprises a spread fence and a high fence - usually a huge, upright wall.

24. The world's fastest breed of horse is a Thoroughbred.

25. The expression is called *Flehmen*.

26. A horse's stomach is as big as a football.

27. False. Ermine markings are black markings on a white leg.

Useful addresses

PONY Magazine
A monthly magazine devoted entirely to horses and ponies - and for horse-mad young people.
D J Murphy (Publishers) Ltd
Haslemere House
Lower Street
Haslemere
Surrey
GU27 2PE
01428 651551

The Pony Club
NAC Stoneleigh Park
Kenilworth
Warwickshire
CV8 2RW
024 7669 8300
Website: www.pcuk.org

Association of British Riding Schools
Queens Chambers
38 - 40 Queen Street
Penzance
Cornwall
TR18 4BH

British Horse Society
Stoneleigh Deer Park
Kenilworth
Warwickshire
CV8 2VX